AUGSBURG OLD TESTAMENT STUDIES

The Message of Job

A Theological Commentary

Daniel J. Simundson

AUGSBURG Publishing House • Minneapolis

THE MESSAGE OF JOB
A Theological Commentary

Copyright © 1986 Augsburg Publishing House

Library of Congress Cataloging-in-Publication Data

Simundson, Daniel J.
THE MESSAGE OF JOB.

(Augsburg Old Testament studies)
Bibliography: p.
1. Bible. O.T. Job—Commentaries.   2. Bible. O.T.
Job—Theology.   I. Title.   II. Series.
BS1415.3.S56   1986   223'.107   86-7893
ISBN 0-8066-2218-0

Manufactured in the U.S.A.   APH 10-4349

1   2   3   4   5   6   7   8   9   0   1   2   3   4   5   6   7   8   9

AUGSBURG OLD TESTAMENT STUDIES

The Message of Jonah by Terence E. Fretheim

The Community and Message of Isaiah 56–66
by Elizabeth Achtemeier

The Message of Exodus by Lester Meyer

The Message of the Psalms by Walter Brueggemann

The Message of Job by Daniel J. Simundson

To Sally

Contents

Editor's Foreword

The *Augsburg Old Testament Studies* series is designed for students of the Bible, especially for pastors and teachers of the community of faith. The volumes have been written with a specific view to the pressing needs of those who use the Bible in the various tasks of ministry. While being responsible to the scholarly study of the Old Testament, the authors seek to address those issues presented by the text in such a way as to touch base with contemporary experience. Seeking to move between technical commentary and preaching guide, they exhibit the influence of the former and the concerns of the latter.

Concentrated attention is given to both the *message* and the *theology* of the biblical material. In using the language of theology, it is recognized that the biblical writers are committed to the God of whom they speak and seek to reflect on the meaning of that reality in their midst. In using the language of message, it is recognized that the biblical writers spoke from faith to faith. They had more than a literary, historical, or even theological focus. To speak of message means that the problems and possibilities of a particular community of faith are in view, and the material has been shaped by attention to such real-life experience.

The complexities and ambiguities of life mean that neither theology nor message can be reduced to formula or dogma or univocal statement. Both must always be on the move with the people in their varying life circumstances, while at the same time being alert to central emphases in the tradition.

Professor Simundson brings to the interpretation of Job a wide range of experience both as an Old Testament teacher/scholar and as a hospital chaplain. The book of Job is thus read through the eyes of one who is thoroughly familiar with the scholarly literature and especially alert to the issues of pastoral care raised by human suffering. The result is a rare combination of Old Testament scholarship and pastoral sensitivity.

Professor Simundson's previous books on suffering (*Faith under Fire: Biblical Interpretations of Suffering* and *Where Is God in My Suffering?* both published by Augsburg) have established his credentials as an interpreter of this dimension of the biblical material. The commentary is thus informed by a considerable range of study in those Old and New Testament texts that relate to the ways in which the people of God have sought to deal with the issues of suffering.

One of the effects of Simundson's experience and expertise is a somewhat different approach to commentary writing. In place of the usual introduction, he immediately delves into issues of suffering raised by the book of Job. He then uses the theme of Job's repentance in 42:6 as a lens through which to view various introductory matters. Moreover, each of the major sections of the commentary concludes with extensive reflections on the theological and pastoral insights that are raised by the texts under consideration. At the same time, his running commentary on the various sections of Job constantly raises concerns that pertain to ways in which suffering should and should not be approached by the people of God today, with just enough detail to keep the reader firmly grounded in the text itself.

This commentary is designed especially for those who would minister to suffering individuals, as well as for those who are struggling with suffering in their own lives. Job's friends are legion. But so, too, are innocent sufferers like Job.

TERENCE E. FRETHEIM

Abbreviations

IB	*Interpreter's Bible.* 12 volumes. Nashville: Abingdon, 1952–1957
IDB	*Interpreter's Dictionary of the Bible.* 4 volumes. Nashville: Abingdon, 1962
IDBSup	Supplementary volume to *IDB.* Nashville: Abingdon, 1976
JB	Jerusalem Bible
JBL	*Journal of Biblical Literature*
KJV	King James Version
NIV	New International Version
RSV	Revised Standard Version
TEV	Today's English Version (Good News Bible)
VT	*Vetus Testamentum*

1

Two Introductory Questions

A. Does Job Deserve This?

When a person as good as Job has to go through horrible suffering, we are puzzled by the seeming inappropriateness of his misfortunes. Good people should not have to endure such catastrophes. In rapid succession, this once successful, wealthy, respected man lost all his wealth, his animals, his servants, and his children. And soon, on top of that, he was afflicted with an ugly and painful disease

What was Job to think? Why was this happening to him? What did he do to deserve this? He was a pious man, a moral man, a good man. And this is the reward he gets.

Job's friends heard about his turn of fortune and came to console him. They, also, were troubled by the severity of his suffering. Could it be that Job deserves this? They had not thought that of Job. Perhaps their earlier assessments of his character had been wrong.

Both Job and his friends had a similar reaction to his suffering. "Did he deserve what had happened to him?" They all started with the same theological point of view. They believed that God will reward the righteous and punish the wicked—within this life. In short, they believed in a doctrine of retribution. Even to raise the question "Does Job deserve this?" already shows a bias, a belief about the origin of suffering, which will have enormous effects on how suffering is borne and how one understands God's participation in the suffering.

The knee-jerk reaction of both Job and his friends to Job's suffering was to assume that he should not have had to suffer unless he deserved it. Suffering is not normal. It is not what God wants for the world. Both Job and his counselors came out of a tradition which assumed a connection between the sins which one commits and the unpleasantness which follows. God is just and powerful and, therefore, the evil and suffering in the world is to be understood in terms of retribution, human fault, punishment for sin.

The belief in a doctrine of retribution is the starting point for looking at the book of Job. Job himself believed in this doctrine. But he was terribly frustrated because it didn't seem to be working. His counselors believed in it but, at least at the beginning, were somewhat puzzled by the apparent blameless character of Job. Many of us religious people continue to fall back on a belief in retribution in times of great trouble. When a friend, a relative, a lovely and pious person faces great pain and suffering, we too ask, "Does she deserve this?" thus giving away our presupposition that that is the way it is supposed to work.

The book of Job is written in response to this common human reaction to suffering, the impulse to seek the cause of the suffering in the sufferer. In our day sufferers continue to censure themselves for their misfortune. It is common to blame the sick, the poor, the oppressed, and the victims of aggression for getting themselves into trouble. Pastors still preach sermons which interpret individual and corporate disasters as God's punishment on a corrupt people. Prayers of confession in our liturgies regularly remind us of a connection between our sinful nature and the trials and tribulations of this life.

The book of Job is still a pertinent word to our generation because we still respond to suffering as if it were retribution for sin. This point of view is very hard to relinquish. For many, as in Job's day, it has become sacred doctrine. There are some reasons for that resistance to let go of this interpretation of suffering. Let us look at a few of them.

Why the belief in a doctrine of retribution is so persistent

1. We have a need to know and control.   Some answer is better than no answer. A doctrine of divine retribution is at least a reasonable explanation for the suffering of the world. And there are not that many alternatives.

The world in which we live is sometimes terrifying, confusing, and uncertain. We live vulnerable lives, subject to illnesses, psychic abuses, and hurts inflicted by others, whether close to us or in halls of judgment at a great distance. If we can make some sense of the world and understand how certain behavior results in certain consequences, perhaps we can gain at least an impression of control over our lives. We can determine what will happen by how we live. We can be successful and avoid suffering, at least up to a point, if we make the right choices. We may even think we have some control over God, since one would expect God to abide by the very rules which God has ordained.

So, we have a great need to find rational meaning even in the chaos of suffering. And we tend to *universalize* what is *sometimes* true. Certainly sinful behavior can lead to suffering. Many biblical texts say that. And obedience to God can lead to a happy life. But it does not necessarily follow that *all* suffering is a result of the sin of the sufferer.

The need for some "answer" to the why of suffering is so strong that many will hang on to a universally applicable doctrine of retribution, even if it means blaming themselves for their trouble. Many think that to abandon this view leaves one with no alternative to the terrifying possibility that there is no sense to it at all. For many, guilt is preferable to meaninglessness.

2. We want to protect God's image as both powerful and good. We need some signs that God is at work in the world. How else can we believe in God? If God acts with power to bring about his purpose, then there ought to be some evidence of that in what happens to people. If faithful followers of God can be destroyed while wicked people continue to prosper, then how can we have any assurance that God is powerful enough to keep God's promises to rule the world with justice? If God never acts on our behalf, then what good is God? If even Job is forced to endure such pain, then how do we know there is a God who is at work in the world, looking out for loved ones and punishing the wicked?

Times of suffering are often occasions of severe strain on one's belief in a good God. A father who has lost a child to a mysterious illness, even though he had implored God to come to her aid, may forever have a sense of doubt about God's willingness and/or ability to act on behalf of those whom God has claimed to love and promised to protect. How can we continue to talk about a God who cares about the world when innocent children die of strange diseases, God's chosen people are massacred in a holocaust, and God's servant Job suffers as if he were the worst of sinners?

For the sake of faith in God, religious apologists often feel compelled to find some way to blame human beings rather than to question God's power or compassion. There is a strong impulse among pious folk to rush to God's defense. So it was with Job's counselors. In spite of evidence to the contrary (Job's life of piety and morality), they retained their belief in retribution. Traditional beliefs about God's involvement in the world were to be protected at the expense of Job's reputation.

3. It is hard to let go of the doctrine of retribution when it has been taught to us as part of our religious tradition. Many people who are very sophisticated in other ways, who may even have abandoned all outward trappings of religious faith (including prayer, Bible reading, and church attendance), will still react to adversity as if God were bringing it as punishment. They had learned that response as children, in Sunday school, in hymns and sermons locked deep in the recesses of their memory, and in biblical texts (from the prophets or the historical books or the sermons of Jesus or the book of Revelation) that pronounce horrible judgments on those who sin.

The traditional understanding of suffering at the time of the writing of the book of Job was that it comes as a result of human sin. The friends of Job knew those answers. They had read their holy writings, the blessings and curses of Deuteronomy, the prophetic interpretation of the destruction of both Israel and Judah. "Who are we to doubt what our ancestors discovered from God and passed on to us? Do we dare set ourselves over against the wisdom of the ages and pretend that, just because we are having a rough time at the moment and we can't make sense out of everything, we know more than the great teachers whom God himself instructed?" As Bildad, the second of Job's counselors, says in Job 8:8-10:

> For inquire, I pray you, of bygone ages, and consider what the fathers have found;
> for we are but of yesterday, and know nothing, for our days on earth are a shadow.
> Will they not teach you, and tell you, and utter words out of their understanding?

The traditional understanding may not always seem to work but, when in doubt, says Bildad, go with the wisdom of the ages. The problem is not with the doctrine, but with your inability to understand it fully.

4. We worry that all ethical motivation will be lost if we relax in our belief in a doctrine of retribution. If belief in rewards and punishment is removed, will people still choose to do the right rather than the wrong? Satan asked that question of God in the first chapter of the book of Job (1:9b), "Does Job serve God for nought?" Satan articulates the cynical view that the only motivation that can inspire people to serve God is the fear of punishment or promise of reward. Take that away and no one will serve God. If this is true, it is very important to maintain belief in a doctrine of retribution.

Satan is not the only one who worries what would happen to the moral life of the world without the fear of punishment. In 15:4, Eliphaz, perhaps the most helpful of the comforters, says to Job, "But you are doing away with the fear of God and hindering meditation before God." In 21:14-15, Job complains to God about the apparent prosperity of the wicked and their refusal to be concerned about God's demands because they are getting away with their evil life-style: "They say to God, 'Depart from us! We do not desire the knowledge of thy ways. What is the Almighty, that we should serve him? And what profit do we get if we pray to him?' "

Is there some other motivation besides retribution that works to persuade one to serve God and other human beings? We hope so. At least we can think of examples of persons who seemed to love God out of pure devotion regardless of unpleasant events in their lives. Is it too cynical to believe that a doctrine of retribution is necessary for morality? Would we behave if not for fear of punishment? Since we Christians tend to project some of our ideas about retribution on to the next life, perhaps we should ask it this way: "Is fear of hell the major motivation for living the Christian life?"

There is obviously much room for difference of opinion on this matter. When should we use the carrot and when the stick? Is capital punishment a deterrent to murder or terrorism? Do strict judges and long prison terms serve as a warning to other possible offenders? At any rate, many believe that a just system of meting out rewards and punishment is absolutely necessary as a motivation for ethical behavior.

For reasons like these, we find it very difficult to give up the doctrine of retribution as a way of understanding human suffering. Even when confronted by seeming cases of innocent suffering, like Job, it is very hard to cut ourselves loose from this belief. Job's counselors could not do it. And in some ways, Job could not either. The effort to maintain the belief in the face of contrary experience led to different problems for each. Job, after all, was the sufferer. The counselors were spectators, observers. Job was on the inside, in the hot seat, the one to whom the doctrine of retribution was being directed. The friends were on the outside, puzzled by the intellectual question, but not facing the threat to their person which confronted Job.

The effect on Job of belief in retribution

A sufferer who believes in the doctrine of retribution is in for a hard time. Job's suffering was compounded by his inability to abandon this understanding of the origin of suffering.

1. Job felt condemned by other human beings. When he most needed love and acceptance from others, those supports were removed. He was a disgrace. He was now poor. He had lost the children who could have provided a kind of immortality as they lived on into the generation after him. There was no one to stand up and speak a good word for him. No one would remember the good man Job and his numerous works on behalf of the needy. Rather, they would forever think of him as the diseased and mournful man who must have done something really awful to deserve such a fate.

Job was not simply imagining this rejection. When his counselors came to talk to him, it soon became clear to him that their estimate of him had changed as a result of his misfortune.

2. A sufferer is driven toward blaming self. That is, of course, the logic of the doctrine of retribution. Job's friends tried to convince Job to look within himself and repent.

Unlike many sufferers, Job refused to accept the blame, though perhaps one can detect a few signs here and there of his wavering from his claims of innocence. With other sufferers, who have less ego strength and more tendency toward self-accusation, a belief in suffering as divine retribution can lead to enormous guilt as they rummage around in their past, looking for anything severe enough to bring on such punishment.

3. God becomes the enemy. Job's relationship with God began to suffer. He began to doubt God's goodness and fairness. If he had been able to look inward and find some cause for his suffering in his own sin, as his counselors suggested to him, the crisis in his relationship with God would possibly have been less severe. But, since he knew he was not guilty, the fault must lie with God. Someone was to blame, and who else is there?

Job never wavered in his belief in God's power. He assumed that if there is a God (and certainly Job never doubted that, even though a modern secular person might in similar circumstances), then God must have power to do what God wants in the world. Since innocent persons (like himself) are suffering and the wicked are not being punished, it follows that there is something gone awry in God's execution of justice. So Job wonders about a God who acts arbitrarily with humans rather than according to the clear lines of the doctrine of retribution.

4. No intellectual answer can fully satisfy a sufferer. The idea of suffering as retribution for sin makes some sense—especially from a distance, from the safety of a quiet study or a relatively comfortable life. It never seems to work quite as well from the perspective of a sufferer on the dung heap. In fact, all intellectual answers sound hollow and insufficient to the person still in the trauma of great suffering. Anyone who has tried to say a word of comfort to one who is suffering knows how trivial, useless, and inappropriate (maybe even offensive) are our feeble attempts to explain to someone else why she or he is suffering. As long as Job was still seeking only *intellectual* answers, definitive statements linking cause and effect, assigning blame to someone for his condition, he was going to be disappointed and frustrated. He was not going to find an answer that worked much better than the one he had learned from his own tradition and which was being presented to him again by his counselors—the doctrine of retribution.

The effect on the counselors of belief in retribution

1. Job's counselors denied experience to protect doctrine. In a situation of seeking to comfort a sufferer, they allowed their doctrine to take precedence over their experience. They had learned that good people are rewarded and wicked people are punished by God in this world. It would be nice if it were so. It would show that God is at work in the world. We would see evidence of that presence and be assured that the world is a moral and sensible place. The problem is that sometimes an event occurs which challenges the authenticity, or at least the universality, of that belief. The case of Job is a prime example. When you look at a person as fine and upstanding and saintly as Job, then you should at least have a few doubts about your neatly devised system for explaining suffering and protecting your idea of God.

But it is hard to let go of theological formulations that have served us well. If the doctrine doesn't fit our experience, then deny the experience, not the doctrine. The doctrine is the absolute to which our experience must conform. We cannot start over in each generation, in each individual life, in each crisis of life. Our personal view is too small. Go with the teachings of your religious tradition even though you are temporarily having some problems fitting them to the current data.

So the doctrine holds. If suffering is the result of sin, then Job must be a sinner, all evidence to the contrary notwithstanding.

2. They put Job in the wrong. That is the inevitable logic of the doctrine of retribution. Whether he looked like a saint or not is beside the point. There must be a sin somewhere. Our task as counselors is to help Job find it. People like Job are even more difficult to deal with than obvious, gross sinners. Job's sins are much more subtle, harder to identify and admit, covered up by superficial acts of piety.

The logic of their position is certain to put the counselors in an adversary relationship with Job. He is convinced that he is innocent. They are sure that he is guilty. He blames God for not being fair. They defend God as always fair. The fault is Job's, not God's. Even to suggest that God is to blame is to reveal some of the sinfulness that is lurking there in Job's mind and heart.

To approach a sufferer, hoping to bring comfort, but believing firmly in divine retribution as the cause of suffering, is to condemn the sufferer before any comfort can be given. We often do this. We condemn those who suffer, as if they brought it on themselves, and by so doing we virtually negate our usefulness as a comforter.

3. The counselors never moved beyond the theoretical level. They did not listen well. They heard Job ask Why? and responded to that. They argued theology. They took the words of a despairing man too seriously, as if they were conducting a seminar on theodicy at the local university.

They should have listened for the despair, the lament, the pain, the fear, and the doubt that lay behind the specific words. They should have acted to meet Job's needs at that level, rather than to argue their theories of retribution. There are times and places for lofty theoretical arguments about the origin of evil. The ash heap of the wounded Job was not the right place.

The doctrine of retribution is the starting point for the actors in the book of Job. It was the prevailing interpretation of suffering at least till the time of Judah's exile. The great poet who gave us this book wanted to say something about the inappropriateness of applying this "answer" to *every* instance of suffering. Job and his counselors start with this traditional belief. The counselors never abandon it. Job, too, is stuck with the residue of this doctrine as he struggles to harmonize it with his own personal integrity. In order to understand much of the dialog between Job and his friends, it is important to keep this context in mind.

B. Why Should Job Repent?

In Job 42:6 Job says, "Therefore, I despise myself and repent in dust and ashes." This word comes at a crucial point and raises many questions about the interpretation of the book of Job. Let us think about the implications of this verse for our study of the book of Job.

Job, the good and faithful man, suffers a series of terrible misfortunes. Three friends come to comfort him, but their words of comfort sound to Job like words of condemnation and, for the major part of the book, Job and his counselors take turns speaking either against one another or past one another. After the intrusion of a fourth counselor, named Elihu, God speaks to Job out of the whirlwind and overwhelms Job with beautiful poetry about the wonders of creation and the inability of humans to comprehend completely the mysteries of the universe. At the close of God's second speech, which takes a similar line, Job seems to become submissive, admits he has been talking about things he had not understood, and declares that he despises himself and repents.

Why should Job repent? Why should he despise himself? At the beginning of the book (1:1; 1:8; 2:3) Job had been singled out because he was blameless, upright, and one who fears God. If all that is true, why should he be in need of repentance? It was Job's counselors who thought that Job deserved his suffering. But those of us who have read the first two chapters of the book and the conclusion (42:7-10) know that it is the counselors who were wrong, not Job. Why then should Job repent?

Many people do not like the picture of a submissive, beaten Job who, though holding onto his integrity and declaring his innocence for a long time, finally cracks under the pressure and comes crawling before God with words of self-hate and repentance. Why should Job repent? The book should not end like this. The tragic, noble, heroic figure of the defiant Job is replaced by the guilt-ridden, typically religious response of giving in to a God who is too powerful to challenge and too mysterious to understand.

By dwelling for a little while on this particular verse (42:6) and the questions which it raises, we can catch a glimpse of some of the major problem areas for students of the book of Job.

Text and translation

Job is probably the most difficult book in the Old Testament to translate (with the possible exception of Hosea). In some places the Hebrew is practically unintelligible. Some scholars have even suggested that it was not originally written in Hebrew, but perhaps was translated into Hebrew (or some form of Hebrew) from Aramaic or Arabic or Edomite or some other language.[1] The text has clearly been corrupted in its transmission. Perhaps a scribe who was not sure of a word changed the text, intending to clarify the meaning but serving only to obscure the original intention of the text all the more. Other scribes coming later would repeat the process and compound the confusion. There are many words which appear nowhere else in the Bible then in Job. There are many unusual grammatical constructions. Further, since it is first-rate poetry, written by an obviously gifted poet, the book sometimes uses vocabulary and images which may be beyond the comprehension of most readers (even in the author's own day, let alone in our time, centuries later). Also, the theological outlook of the book of Job and its direct accusations toward God would surely cause some orthodox readers to cringe—and perhaps even to tone down some of Job's more daring outbursts. This can be seen by comparing some ancient translations of Job (like the Greek) with the Hebrew.[2] In fact, the Greek version of Job is very different from the Hebrew, being considerably shorter in the poetic sections.

The point is that there are many passages in Job which are not clearly translatable. What we read in our English translation may be only an educated guess. Our modern translations indicate at many points that the meaning of the Hebrew is uncertain (e.g., the notes to Job 19:26 in the RSV).

Let us return to our example—42:6. Even though the Hebrew words in this verse are well known, there are still some difficulties about what the verse actually means. There is no object for the Hebrew word *despise*. The Hebrew simply reads, "Therefore, I despise," or "I loathe," or "I reject." We are not told what it is that Job rejects. Is it himself (as in the RSV)? Is it the presumtuous words he has been uttering (as in the JB)? Has he now finally rejected his angry and complaining posture of lamenting?[3] Some have even dared to suggest that Job is here expressing loathing toward God.[4] In a case like this, a translator will try to understand the context and will make an educated guess about what is actually meant.

Further, in the last half of the verse, Job says that he "repents" in dust and ashes. The Hebrew word translated "repent" in this case (*niham*) is not the usual word that is used for human repentance (that word is *šûb*) when a person turns away from former ways and comes anew before God. The Hebrew word *niham* has the meaning of being sorry or relenting or even of being comforted. When these factors are all examined together, one sees that the meaning of the text may be much more complicated than the customary "Therefore I despise myself and repent in dust and ashes."[5] No doubt Job takes back, abandons, or regrets things he has said or done, but the word *repent* probably overstates the idea of his sinfulness.

So there are problems of translation even in a text like this, where the Hebrew words are well known and there seems little evidence of corruption in transmission. The Septuagint (the earliest Greek version) does not translate the Hebrew precisely and gives evidence that even that ancient translator struggled with what the text intended to say.

With most passages in Job, textual problems are not determinative for the meaning. We can get the idea of the message, the feel of it, the overall sense. The problem becomes more acute with a pivotal verse like 42:6, which many see as the climax of the whole book. If this is so, and we cannot be sure what is meant, then we obviously have some problems understanding the basic intention of the book. Another example of a crucial passage which is difficult to translate is the famous "for I know that my Redeemer lives" passage (19:25-26).

As we read the book of Job, it is important to bear in mind the unique textual problems of this biblical book. We will ignore most of them, basing our comments on the RSV. One could spend a lifetime—and more—delving into the problems of the text of Job; we will leave that task to others. Only occasionally—when they seem to be of particular relevance—will we bring up textual questions.

The unity of the book of Job

Our verse (42:6) raises the question of the unity of the book of Job. If Job had been declared blameless by God in the opening chapters of the book, then why must Job repent? Further, in the passage immediately following our verse, the counselors, not Job, have not spoken what is right. Is this an inconsistency? Many have thought so and have attempted to make sense of this, and other inconsistencies, by hypothesizing that the book of Job was not written as a complete unit by one author at one time.

The most obvious division is between the prose sections (the introduction, Chaps. 1–2, and the conclusion, 42:7-17) and the body of the book, which is written in poetry. Nearly everyone has noted differences between the prose and poetry of the book of Job. The prose account assumes Job is innocent. But at the end of the poetic section he is brought to repentance (our verse, 42:6). The proverbial "patient Job" is found only in the prose section, certainly not in the poetic section. The prose account seems detached, almost coldly indifferent to the suffering of Job, but the poetic section shows a passionate and intimate understanding of what it is to suffer. The prolog and epilog (the prose sections) provide some limited reasons for suffering, but there are no rational answers for Job (or the reader) in the poetry.

For these and other reasons, most scholars have concluded that the story of Job in the prolog and epilog is not an original unit with the rest of the book. The possibilities of how they came together in their present form include the following: *(a)* the author of the poetry also wrote the prose, but perhaps at a different time and deliberately in a different style; *(b)* a prose narrative existed separately from the poetry and at some point an editor (who did not write any of it) brought the two together; *(c)* the prose narrative existed prior to the writing of the present book of Job and was used by a poetic genius to frame his great work. This last hypothesis seems the most reasonable to me and is probably the one most commonly accepted by students of Job.[6]

So it appears that there were at least two steps in the development of the book of Job as it appears in our Bibles. First, there was an ancient tale about an innocent sufferer. Second, there was an extended poetic work inserted in the middle of the ancient tale; this contained impassioned outbursts by Job, words of comfort and advice by three friends, and separate responses from Job, all of which was climaxed by a long-hoped-for confrontation between Job and God. Following this appearance by God, Job repents in dust and ashes, and there is a quick return to the epilog and a rounding out of the story.

Most scholars also believe that there is a third stage in the formation of the book of Job. In Chaps. 32–37 a fourth counselor appears. He had not been heard from prior to this time. He is not mentioned in the prolog or epilog (where reference is made to the other three) and appears nowhere else in the poetic sections. His words are appreciated by some commentators but relegated to secondary importance by most. Almost everyone considers these chapters to be an intrusion, a later effort by someone to make further comments on the book of Job, to try to say more convincingly what had already been said, and to lean a little more heavily on the idea that suffering can have educative value for us.[7]

So we have three stages in the development of our biblical book. There have also been suggestions that other chapters (especially Chap. 28 and parts or all of God's speeches) are secondary additions to the original poem. We shall make further note of these points when we look at those sections of Job. Here it is enough to say that there are good reasons to believe that the present book of Job is not a unity in the sense that the whole book originated at the same time from the hand of one author. It is passages like 42:6 ("Why should Job repent if he is as blameless as God said he was in 1:8 or 42:7?") which have raised the questions that scholars have attempted to answer with theories of stages in the development of the book of Job.

Outline of the book of Job

1–2	Prolog
3	Job's passionate outburst
4–27	Three cycles of speeches of three visitors and responses from Job
28	A poem about the inaccessibility of wisdom
29–31	Job's concluding statement—longing for old days and oath of innocence
32–37	Elihu's speeches
38–41	Two speeches by God
40:3-5	Job's reply to God's first speech
42:1-6	Job's response to God's second speech
42:7-17	Epilog

The book is framed by the prolog and epilog. As suggested earlier, perhaps there was an ancient tale which was used by the author. After setting forth the story of Job's situation and introducing Job's three friends, the book of Job takes a long poetic excursion into a presentation of ideas on the meaning of suffering and Job's reactions to those explanations of why there is suffering in the world and why it hits some people and not others. At the close of this lengthy discussion, God finally speaks—after being silent through all the discussions (at least from Job's perspective, since he did not know about the conversations going on in heaven). The book then closes with the epilog, another prose section, very similar in style to the opening two chapters, in which Job's prosperity returns and he again leads a satisfying life, surrounded by a new family into a very old age.

The main part of the book of Job is in the form of three cycles of speeches. Each of Job's three friends speaks in turn, followed in each case by a word from Job. After they each have spoken, they start all over again until the cycle is repeated three times. The third cycle is in some disorder. Job says what we would expect to hear from one of the counselors and one of the friends is not mentioned at all. We shall say more about this when we look at that part of the book.

The section containing the three cycles begins and ends with speeches by Job. In Chap. 3 Job utters a powerful lament, thereby opening up the discussion and probably stirring many thoughts and feelings within his counselors. When the three cycles are completed, Job again speaks, bringing the conversation with his friends to a close, reminiscing about the good days before his present troubles began, and declaring again his innocence of any crime severe enough to bring on the calamities which had befallen him.

Two sections seem to intrude in this rather nicely balanced, symmetrical structure: Chap. 28 on wisdom and Elihu's speeches in Chaps. 32–37. Elihu's speeches are almost surely a later addition, whether by the author or (more likely) by a later hand. It is more difficult to know where the poem about wisdom came from, why it was inserted here, and who put it here.

The meaning of the book of Job

Job 42:6 is a very important verse for studying the meaning of the book of Job, the intention of the great poet who used an ancient story for his starting point. It comes at the end of Job's response to his confrontation with God. It is the end of the poetic section. If it is so important, then, what did the poet mean? Why should Job repent? The way we answer that question will go a long way in revealing how we understand the book of Job. Further, it may show how we understand suffering in general, how we would respond to suffering in our own lives, and how we react to the sufferers we encounter.

The reader of Job finds it very difficult to be completely objective about the meaning of the book. Suffering is a subject with which most people have had some experience, and they bring their own questions and solutions to the task of interpretation. Some people are angered by the way God talks to Job in Chaps. 38–41. They think God has unfairly browbeaten poor Job and, therefore, they are disappointed with Job's reaction of denouncing himself and repenting. Other people are anxious to defend God and to find some moral and just reason why God allowed Job to suffer (even if they have to fall back on the doctrine of retribution). Perhaps, as Job's counselors suggested, Job really did deserve his suffering. Or at least he *needed* it ("Thanks, God, I needed that!") in order to become a better person. In general, those who read Job from a religious orientation are less bothered by Job's submission to God at the end than those readers who have thought of Job as a heroic figure who is unwilling to give in to his terrible fate.

According to the first two chapters, Job is an innocent sufferer. Yet, in 42:6, Job despises himself and repents. One can deal with this discrepancy, as we have suggested, by looking again at the Hebrew text and hypothesizing that it does not actually mean what most translators have thought it meant. Perhaps the religious orientation of the translators has influenced them in their picture of a pious, repentant, submissive Job, even though the text itself is not that certain.

Another way to deal with this disharmony between Chaps. 1–2 and 42:6 is to suggest that we have different sources. The common solution is to suppose that there was an ancient story, already in circulation in written form, which was used by the author of the poetry as a jumping-off point for his discussion. Therefore, the poet may not be personally responsible for all the views expressed in the prolog, but rather is stuck with an already-existent story which he cannot change.

Though I agree that it makes good sense to postulate several stages in the formation of the book of Job, it seems too simple to dismiss all apparent contradictions on the basis of hypothetical sources. On a subject as complicated as the meaning of human suffering, there is no simple solution, and our poet never intends to suggest one. We may be left with contradictions, ambiguities, unanswered questions, and illogical conclusions simply because of the nature of the question. At some point, our present book of Job emerged as we know it, so someone apparently thought that it was all right to combine the prose and poetic sections without destroying the message of the book.

So, why should Job repent? Surely we must hold fast to the repudiation of the doctrine of retribution in the case of Job. Job is not suffering because of any wrong he has committed. His need for repentance, then, must be a consequence of some things about himself which were uncovered by his suffering. The problem was in his reaction to his suffering, not that he deserved his suffering. Think with me about a few possible reasons why Job should repent.

1. Job needed a visible sign of God's blessing and concern. Job expected—and even demanded—evidence of God's love. Job tied earthly success to his beliefs about a good God. If God loved him, then Job should be well. If God cared about him, he should not have to endure suffering, lose his wealth, and grieve over his children. In a sense, Job was putting God to the test. "If you love me, God, show me." Job had thought that you know about God by looking at the things God does for you. A good God does good things to those who deserve them. If it does not work that way, then how can we know anything about God?

Many have had the same problem as Job. Many religious people who have expected always to have things work out well for them have had to deal with great disillusionment at times of suffering. Many believe that their faith in God will somehow lead to an easier, relatively pain-free life. When that doesn't happen, they begin to wonder about God. Religions that promise great earthly rewards as evidence of God's presence among the faithful can survive as long as everything goes well, the healing takes place, the job is rewarding, the rebellious children come home, and "positive thinking" works. The flaw in such a religion shows up when disaster strikes, when a "winner" suddenly becomes a "loser," when the sickness leads not to healing but to chronic suffering or death. Is God there in the suffering? If one needs visible signs of God's bounty in order to believe in a good God, then how do you find God at those low times when your need for the comfort of the Almighty is the most intense?

2. God became an enemy to Job. More and more Job began to think of God as an adversary, someone who was pulling strings in order to bring on this suffering. He assumed God had the power to make things happen in the world, and he was reasonably certain that he did not deserve what was happening to him (especially when he looked around and compared himself with other people). Since what was happening to him was bad, Job blamed God for his troubles.

Perhaps Job needed to repent because he had come to think of God as a punisher, an avenger, a tormenter, an enemy. With such an attitude toward God, Job was inconsolable. He needed to repent, to change his mind, before he could come to think of God again as a friend, a comforter, one to whom he could turn for help in times of suffering.

This often happens to sufferers. God becomes the enemy. God is blamed for whatever happens to us. No matter where the suffering comes from (for example, a car accident in which a drunk driver recklessly runs into our car), God is blamed because God is God and should have had the power to prevent it. The first reaction of many sufferers is to cry out in anger to God. God is causing, or at least allowing, my trouble. How can you turn to God for comfort when you are blaming God for your trouble? Some "believers" turn away in disgust or find it difficult to believe in God at all. Job continued to believe in God, though, to be sure, his view of God as enemy had distorted his ability to find comfort in that belief. Perhaps it is this distortion which called for repentance.

3. Job carried the lament too far.   We shall refer more to lament as we go through the book of Job. Job was, some may think, too negative, preoccupied with self, groveling in self-pity, too direct in his accusations toward God.

There is a great tendency in Christianity and in our culture to stifle lament. Those who feel that *any* lamenting is a mistake, who feel that we must turn away from negative thoughts and fill our minds only with positive ones, will probably be convinced that Job should repent because he has gotten himself into such a negative state that he can never get out unless he changes his attitude. A little lamenting is OK—maybe, or for a little while. Most people need to blow off a little steam, to work through the process of facing reality when unpleasantness comes into their lives. But Job goes too far—cursing the day of his birth, screaming at God and his counselors, feeling excessively sorry for himself.

Perhaps Job did overreact. Some students of the book have come to that conclusion. Maybe that is a valid reason for his repentance. On the other hand, how can you tell men and women that they should stop lamenting, that it has lasted long enough, that it has almost overstepped the bounds of proper address to God, when they (the ones actually suffering) still feel that they have more lamenting to do? Whose timetable are people supposed to be working on? Some mourners may grieve the loss of a loved one for years. Others may pass through this stage much more quickly. So it took Job a little longer than some to settle down and accept his misfortunes and quit complaining about them. But is that any reason to despise oneself and repent in dust and ashes?

4. Job lacked humility.   This is probably the most common way of answering our question why Job should repent. Though he certainly did not appear to be a sinner, Job, like all other humans, suffered from pride. Often it is the good people like Job who have the hardest time recognizing that they are sinful human beings. Job's counselors suggested that Job was not as good a person as he thought he was and that, under the pressure of suffering, his true colors were beginning to show. Many interpreters of Job seem to have joined the comforters in trying to find some hidden sin of Job which might justify his suffering after all. Perhaps his greatest sin was his overconfidence about his innocence.

Human pride also shows up in the way Job pursued his questions. He assumed that human beings should be able to find intellectually satisfying solutions if they search long enough. When his friends failed to provide answers, Job demanded to hear from God himself. "Tell me why I am suffering, God. There must be a reason. I want to know what it is. Tell me."

Maybe Job needs to repent simply for raising these questions in the first place. Humans are never satisfied to live with uncertainties, unanswered questions. They want to know more. They even want to know what God knows so that they will not have to remain dependent creatures, forced to trust God in those areas where human beings will never have complete knowledge. If we could only find convincing arguments that would settle our questions about God once and for all!

Perhaps Job needed to be humbled. God never really answered his questions and, in fact, made it clear that humans will simply have to resign themselves to a certain degree of ignorance. So, maybe that is Job's problem, his need to repent. He is too presumptuous, too confident in human reason, deluding himself into the thought that he can approach God as an equal (31:37b, "like a prince I would approach him"), not willing to give up the search for intellectual answers and throw himself on the mercy of God.

All of this is probably true. Yet I worry about giving up the search too soon, or giving advice to other people that it is time to *stop* thinking and *start* believing. There is a lot of anti-intellectualism around in the church and in our society which is destructive of human dignity and curiosity. Many people do not like the way the book of Job ends because they think it concludes with a great put-down of the human intellectual enterprise. If it is ultimately all a matter of faith, then why do we waste so much of our time and energy thinking about questions which will always remain beyond our capacity to comprehend?

Timing here is very important. It can be very cruel to demand that someone stop asking questions too soon (like a teenager in a confirmation class or a person still deeply in need of more time to lament). We all have different credibility levels. Some can believe easier and faster than others. The reality of a good God can never be proved. But some of us, like Job, have to work a little harder before we are finally ready to admit that.

5. Job's religion was secondhand, not personal. Job had thought that he knew something about God and human suffering. He had even been a counselor himself, giving words of comfort and advice to others. But when his own private world fell apart, the old answers that he had been using did not help any more. In fact, they seemed almost to drive him farther from God.

He had been going on hearsay, secondhand religion, what he had learned from others, rather than from his own deepest spiritual experience. One could hardly blame him for that. Like all of us, Job had learned his religion from his religious community and appropriated it for himself as his life unfolded.

With new experiences of life, new understandings and challenges to his faith would come. In his time of suffering, the old answers no longer worked and he did not know how to find the good God that he used to know. He needed a firsthand experience of God. Though he talked as if he wanted an intellectual answer to his questions about his suffering, what he really needed was a personal assurance of God's presence and concern.

When that experience came, God speaking from the whirlwind, the sudden awareness of being in the presence of God could have driven Job to his knees in repentance. This often happened to people in the Bible when they were confronted by God. In the verse immediately prior to the one we have been examining, Job says, "I had heard of thee by the hearing of the ear, but now my eye sees thee" (42:5).

Job wanted an encounter with God. But he could not make it happen. It finally came when God himself came to Job. Neither can we make it happen to suit our own timetable—either in our own lives or the lives of those we are trying to comfort.

6. Job was often hostile toward other people.   Maybe his awareness of that, following his confrontation with God, is what precipitated his mood of repentance.

He was terribly impolite, if not actually rude, to the friends who had come with the intention of bringing him some consolation. No one likes to be insulted the way Job castigated them. Further, Job (as well as his friends) discussed the "wicked" people almost as if they were abstractions instead of real flesh-and-blood persons whom God loved. Job claimed that he was innocent and, as we often do, sought to make his point stronger by comparing himself to others who were more easily identifiable as sinners. For Job, it was an example of God's failure to execute justice that such unsavory people should be allowed to go through life without being properly punished. It almost sounds as if Job is angry because those people are not suffering, as if he can hardly wait till they get theirs (it reminds you how some Christians seem to enjoy talking about those other folks who are going to hell).

Perhaps this is Job's problem, his need to repent: he does not love other people. Doesn't he know that God cares about sinners, too? Often the religious person does not want God to be too easy on the offender. "Make them pay. Don't let them off the hook. If you're too easy on them, God, it will set a bad example for those of us who are busting our backs trying to do what we are supposed to do." If this is Job's problem, it certainly is one that is common to religious people. We are reminded of the "older brother" in the parable of the prodigal son or Jonah, who spoke words of judgment on Nineveh and was upset with God when God decided to forgive them instead of bringing the judgment which Jonah had proclaimed.

Why did Job have the need to repent? What defect or wrong attitude or sin showed up in his time of suffering which needed changing? Did he become a better person because of the suffering which he endured and the repentance to which he finally came? Perhaps. There may be some truth to all of our suggested explanations for his repentance. At any rate, they raise for us major questions to keep in the back of our minds as we read through the book of Job.

One closing word of caution: We need to watch out for our tendency to find some fault in the sufferer, something that needs punishing, correcting, disciplining. We so easily revert to some variation of a doctrine of retribution (though perhaps a more subtle one than that propagated by Job's friends) in which sufferers must be held responsible for their own troubles and God cannot in any way be blamed. Sufferers, ancient ones like Job and those in our own day, often feel that they are being blamed for their own suffering. "If Job needed to repent, is it possible that he brought the suffering on himself after all?" Very subtly, without being fully aware, we may have drifted to the side of Job's counselors—blaming him and defending God. And by so doing, we have lost the deeper meaning of the book of Job.

2

The Prolog
(Job 1-2)

Let us now go to the beginning of the book of Job and move through it in order. As we have mentioned, the first two chapters, usually called the prolog, set the stage for all that follows.

The Prolog

The prolog is written in good Hebrew prose. In contrast to the difficult text of the poetry, the first two chapters of Job can be read rather easily by anyone who has a fair knowledge of Hebrew. It reminds one of the stories in earlier books of the Old Testament, such as Genesis, Judges, or Ruth. This makes it very difficult to date this part of Job with any feeling of confidence. Some have thought that it was written very early because of its style and its similarity with older parts of the Bible. Job is mentioned in Ezek. 14:14,20 as if he were an ancient figure well known in the first half of the sixth century B.C.E. So it seems that there was a story about someone named Job at least before the exile, and maybe much before. Some have proposed that the story in its present form may not be so old. Its apparent age may be a deliberate effort to rewrite the story of Job in the style of the stories known in the books of Moses and the historical books.[8]

In the two chapters of the prolog we have five separate scenes. Three take place on earth and two tell of events occurring beyond human perception in heaven. The first scene (1:1-5) introduces us to Job and tells us some very significant things about him. The second scene switches to heaven for a conversation between God and Satan (1:6-12), followed by the first round of calamities for Job in scene three (1:13-22). There follows a second scene between God and Satan, in which it is determined that a further testing will take place (2:1-6). This is followed by the final scene, where Job, now stricken with a vicious disease, continues to resist the temptation to curse God (2:7-10). At the close of this scene, Job's three friends are introduced (2:11-13) to prepare the reader for the poetic sections which follow.

The good man Job (1:1-5)

Job was from Uz, a place difficult to locate, but certainly outside Israel.[9] It is worth noting that neither Job nor his friends were Israelites. They were foreigners. The problems of suffering know no ethnic nor geographic boundaries. We are dealing with a common human question with which every culture and every religion must come to terms. Some scholars have noted similarities between the biblical Job and other stories about innocent or meaningless suffering in the ancient Near East.[10] It is not necessary to postulate direct borrowing from any of these stories by the biblical writer. Whatever seems similar can be explained from the commonality of human experience and parallel efforts to understand a world which does not always conform to our expectations.

In the very first verse of the book we are told that Job was "blameless and upright" and "feared God and turned away from evil." God confirms this judgment on Job in his conversations with Satan in 1:8 and 2:3. This is a crucial point for the understanding of the book of Job and it is made right at the beginning. There is no doubt that Job does not deserve the suffering which he is about to endure. God himself has declared Job to be the best human being that one could find, a paragon of virtue, morally sound and religiously faithful. It is necessary for those of us who read the book of Job to know this about its chief character. If we were to begin the book of Job with the dialogs between Job and his friends (that is, without the prolog), we would not know whether Job was right in protesting his innocence or whether the counselors were right in upholding the doctrine of retribution and looking for some secret sin in the man. The prolog is necessary to the rest of the book, whether or not it was written by the same author as the rest of the book, because it makes it absolutely clear that Job is a case of innocent suffering.

Job himself is, of course, in the dark about why he is suffering. He does not know what God is doing in heaven. Like all humans, he is not given details of the decisions made in God's heavenly court, even when those decisions affect him personally.

Job was a man of great wealth, not least of which was his family of seven sons and three daughters (1:2-3). Those sons took turns hosting joyous feasts, to which the daughters were also invited. The text seems to be painting the picture of happiness, joy, comfort, love, and all good things that one would want from life. Perhaps a stern critic of society (like Amos) might read this text and begin to wonder about these offspring of Job. Were they so busy partying that they had no socially useful work to do? Were they squandering their obvious wealth, while many people around them were in desperate need? Are they examples of the idle rich, the "beautiful people" of their day? One of Job's counselors, Bildad in 8:4, will suggest some fault on the part of Job's children, but the text seems not to say that. We should not follow Bildad's temptation to look for some defect in the children which would help give a moral justification for their destruction.

The last verse (1:5) raises some intriguing questions about Job and how he thought about God in those good days before his troubles started. Why is he so careful, so scrupulous, so compulsive about carrying out this ritual with regard to his sons? One wonders about his almost mechanistic belief in the efficacy of ritual sacrifice. On the one hand, Job lives in fear that all has not been done properly and God might find some flaw for which punishment will be the inevitable consequence. On the other hand, he may have been lulled into a false sense of security by this way of thinking, as if by doing all things properly one can achieve control over the events in one's life—even a guarantee that suffering can be avoided.

Probably, the author includes this bit of information about Job's offerings on behalf of his sons in order to emphasize that there is no possible doubt about Job. All bases have been covered. As far as the doctrine of retribution is concerned, Job has dealt with all questions, tied every loophole, sealed every crack. If ever someone could expect to avoid suffering by proper living, Job should have made it. Not only outward actions are taken into consideration, but even hypothetical unpleasant thoughts toward God by his sons are forgiven through the proper ritual. Job cannot be held accountable even for the possible "inner" sins of his sons because he has taken the caution to deal with them in the way provided by his religious traditions. Job is clean. He is innocent. He does not deserve to suffer.

The RSV translates v. 5b, "It may be that my sons have sinned, and cursed God in their hearts." The word translated "cursed" is actually the Hebrew word "blessed." There are seven places in the Old Testament where the RSV translates the word that usually means "bless" into the opposite meaning of "curse." Four of these examples are in the first two chapters of Job (1:5,11 and 2:5,9). Two are in the story of Naboth's vineyard in 1 Kings 21:10,13, and the other is in Ps. 10:3. The same Hebrew word occurs one other time in these chapters where it is translated with its usual meaning: "*Blessed* be the name of the Lord" (1:21c).

This points out for us again the difficulty of translating an ancient document into our own language. We want to take the Bible literally and choose English words which are precise equivalents of the Hebrew. In these four occurrences in Job 1–2, however, the usual translation, "bless," makes no sense. The context indicates something like "curse," or "blaspheme," or "renounce," and our English translations have chosen words like those even though they are not conveying the common literal meaning of the Hebrew words.

How does a word come to mean its exact opposite? Probably it has to do with religious sensitivities about the name of God. Even to link a word like "curse" with God is to show disrespect and irreverence. The question remains whether this was a euphemism used by the author—substituting a less offensive word for the impious term—or whether it was later copyists of the book who softened potentially blasphemous language.[11] Further, we do not know if this was a euphemism in general use so that readers would understand that it meant something other than its literal meaning. The similar passage in 1 Kings 21 might support that possibility, though that is not enough evidence to make a strong case. At any rate, though my inclination is to accept the meaning "curse," I remain a little uncertain whether we really understand fully what is meant here.

God and Satan talk about Job (1:6-12)

The scene now shifts to the heavenly court. It is a day when the "sons of God" appear before God. Since the poet has not been there to observe what goes on in heaven, he uses his poetic imagination and describes it as similar to what would take place in a king's court, where ambassadors and other officials present themselves to report to the king. The "sons of God" are heavenly beings, part of the heavenly hosts, what we might speak of as angels. Satan seems to be some such being. He is not outwardly hostile to God (though he raises questions which probably have evil intent), but rather seems to be a roving ambassador who keeps an eye on what is going on in the world and then comes back to the court from time to time to give his report.

In v. 8, God brings up the subject of Job. God boasts about what a fine person Job is and wonders if Satan had also noticed Job. One could speculate what would have happened to Job if God had not chosen to make such a point of how good he was. Would Job have continued with his good life as described in 1:1-5, finally coming into a pleasant old age without having to endure all the sufferings that were precipitated by God bringing his name to Satan's attention? One might deduce from this that it would be better not to be so outstanding that you are noticed by God. Better to be lost in the crowd than to be singled out as a special test case, the arena for resolution of an argument between God and Satan.

Satan's response to God's appreciative words about Job is the question "Does Job fear God for nought?" (v. 9). God has protected Job from every danger and has brought him prosperity. Why shouldn't Job be faithful to God? He would be a fool not to. He has everything going his way. His devotion to God has never been tested. What would he do if his good life were taken away? Satan suggests that Job would curse God to his face (v. 11). Satan implies that Job's motivation for serving God is purely self-serving. Take away the rewards and the motivation will disappear. Such cynical accusations have often been made about those who seem to be good persons, who do good deeds for others, who remain loyal to God and strive to fulfill his demands. Like Satan, many have suggested that the religious person is not motivated by love of God but by concern for self, whether it be a longing for rewards and the avoidance of unpleasantness in this life or the promise of heaven and avoidance of hell in the next life. This is an important question that Satan raises—so important, in fact, that God is moved to allow Satan to put his theory to the test. God permits Job to come under Satan's power, with the one stipulation that Job himself is not to be harmed.

Job loses wealth and family, but holds firm (1:13-22)

Disasters come to Job in rapid succession. There is much repetition in vv. 13-19 as one messenger after another comes to tell of some new catastrophe. Before one carrier of grim tidings has even finished getting the words out of his mouth, another one has come knocking at the door. The bad news comes in four stages: an attack from the Sabeans (v. 15), fire of God from heaven (v. 16), a raid by the Chaldeans (v. 17), and a great wind (v. 19). Along the way, Job loses all of his animals, his servants, and, finally, his children. Two of the disasters are the work of human enemies and two come from natural causes (probably a lightning storm and a whirlwind). Whether the trouble comes from other human beings (Sabeans and Chaldeans) or from the powerful outbreak of natural disasters, Satan somehow has influenced what has taken place.

The piling up of such grim events in such a short time would be almost comical if it were not so tragic. In a brief moment of time, Job has been reduced from a wealthy and honored and happy man to a poor and unhappy man, bereft of the comforts and honor that wealth can bring and deprived of the serenity about the future that belongs to those who know they have offspring to carry on their seed into the next generation. Job's loss was enormous. What is he to think about God now?

Job held firm. He reacted with the appropriate ritual of mourning (v. 20) and continued to worship God (v. 20b). He came forth from his mother's womb naked and would return the same way (the meaning probably is that he came into the world without any possessions and would also leave without anything; "You can't take it with you"). Job is still submissive to God and is willing to part with his blessings because they were all gifts anyway. It is the Lord who gives, and thus it is the Lord who has the right to take away. God is still blessed in Job's view, in spite of everything.

If Satan expected Job to turn on God and denounce him because of his misfortune, Job had shown that Satan was wrong. Job continues to worship God even without the rewards he had been receiving.

Satan gets another chance (2:1-6)

Again the scene shifts back to heaven. The setting is the same as the earlier one, with the "sons of God" coming before God. Once again, God brings up the subject of Job. God affirms once more the fact that there is no one on earth who can compare with Job as a blameless, upright, God-fearing person. Further, God is obviously pleased about the way that Job has held up during the harassment from Satan. "He [Job] still holds fast his integrity, although you moved me against him to destroy him *without cause.*" The Hebrew word translated "without cause" here is the same word which was uttered by Satan in 1:9, "Does Job fear God *for nought?*" God had been persuaded by Satan to allow Job to endure suffering. We might say that God did not actually do evil to Job, but God did allow it. God seems here to acknowledge his part in permitting Job's sufferings, even admitting that the suffering was "without cause." Job had put up with a lot of agony already (not to mention what the slain servants and sons and daughters had to endure) for "no good reason" (another translation of "without cause").

Satan is not ready to quit yet. True, Job has been tested. But you don't really know what suffering is until it strikes your own body. Physical pain and deterioration, the looks of horror on others as they see how your physical appearance has changed, the agonizing constant ache that never goes away, the fear of losing life itself—let's see how Job handles that. It is one thing to suffer the loss of wealth or even the death of loved ones, but the real crunch comes when one's own self is under attack. "We haven't made the test hard enough yet," says Satan. "Touch his bone and flesh and he will show his true colors, abandon his pious pretensions, and end up cursing God."

Once again God is persuaded by this argument and God allows Satan to proceed with his dirty work. Job again is in Satan's power. There is still one stipulation, however. Satan is not allowed to kill Job (2:6). As we shall see later in the book, there were times when Job would have preferred that this limitation not be in force so that he could die and be rid of the suffering.

Job is sick, but still faithful (2:7-13)

This time suffering affects Job in a very direct and personal way. He is afflicted with a horrible disease in which he is covered with sores from his head to the soles of his feet. He sits in the garbage dump, scraping his sores, in great pain (vv. 7-8).

At this point in the story, Job's wife appears on the scene. She says to Job, "Curse God, and die" (2:9b). What does she mean by this? Why would she say such a thing? Job's wife is an intriguing figure. We wish we knew more about her. Even what we read here is ambiguous—we cannot be sure what is intended. Is she working in cooperation with Satan, whose goal is to get Job to curse God (remember what we have already said about the use of a word that usually means "bless" to convey a meaning that appears to be "curse")? That has been a common interpretation of this passage throughout the years, linking Job's wife with Eve and Delilah and Jezebel and other temptresses who have worked with Satan to lead good men into acts of self-destruction. Such interpretations have been part of the church's teaching. They have recently become very troublesome to those who are trying to rethink the church's positions on the role of women.

One could just as well argue that Job's wife is speaking out of compassion for the man she loves. She is so desperately moved by his suffering that she hopes that he will die and not suffer any more. Many husbands or wives or sons or daughters have stood over the bed of their tormented loved ones and had similar thoughts. If cursing God will bring the final end quicker, then perhaps Job should curse and get it over with. If God is to blame for what has happened to Job, then perhaps God should be cursed. A woman who loves her husband deeply might even be angry enough at God and so in empathy with the suffering spouse that she would dare to say such things to God himself. People in the Bible do challenge God and get angry with God and argue with God. At any rate, let us not be too harsh in making a negative judgment about Job's wife, especially when we see how her story has been linked with other stories to paint a stereotyped and condemning picture of women which has persisted in some areas of the church up to the present time.

In v. 10 Job does rebuke his wife. He claims that she is speaking "as one of the foolish women would speak." Again it is left to the imagination of the interpreter to conjecture exactly what is meant by that. In our day, some have suggested that here we have a classic contrast between a stoic man and a woman who is able to express her emotions. At any rate, Job is not going to protest. He is not going to curse God. He is not going to say anything critical about God. He will take it "like a man." He says, "Shall we receive good at the hand of God, and shall we not receive evil?" (2:10b). God is the ultimate authority. Therefore, "whatever God chooses to bring upon me, I will take, whether it is something that seems to be good or seems to be evil."

Satan has applied the screws to Job twice. Job survives, still persisting in his allegiance to God. He appears to be the model of a religious person, so confident in God's ultimate plan that he will not protest or doubt God even when his world goes to hell in a basket. Job hangs in there and says the right religious words. Satan surely must have been disappointed.

At the close of the prolog, we are introduced to Job's three friends (vv. 11-13). This brief passage is a crucial transition to the poetic sections which follow. Even if the poet of the book of Job used an ancient story that was written by someone else, he must have shaped these few verses to make the link with the rest of the book.

Eliphaz, Bildad, and Zophar made an appointment with each other to come together to comfort Job (2:11b). In light of their subsequent failure to bring him comfort, we should remember that their motivation was a good one. They did care about Job and were deeply moved by his situation. When they first saw him, they were so affected by his appearance that they wept. His illness had changed him so that they did not even recognize him (v. 12a). It is a terribly disturbing experience to see a close friend or loved one so devastated by illness (such as cancer) that you hardly recognize anymore the one that you used to know so well.

For a whole week, these friends sat with Job without saying a word (2:13). That is hard for us to imagine. In our day we are largely intolerant of long periods of silence. When we call upon a sufferer, we are usually gripped with a compulsion to say something, to try to bring a word of comfort or insight. The silence only seems to emphasize our helplessness in the face of most pains and sufferings in our world. Some commentators have noted that Job's friends were most helpful to him during the seven days in which they had the wisdom to say nothing. That was the best counseling that they did. When Job began to speak, and the counselors began to argue theology with him, they were not much help anymore. If we wish to learn anything positive about being a comforter from the friends of Job, we had best look at their seven days of silence, not at the discussions which follow.

THEOLOGICAL AND PASTORAL IMPLICATIONS

There are several questions that arise from our look at the first two chapters of Job which deserve a few more words of comment.

1. Is there such a thing as innocent suffering?

The first two chapters of Job speak a resounding yes to this question. Job is certainly written to counteract an oversimplified doctrine of retribution which rather too neatly points to connections between the sin one commits and the suffering one experiences. To be sure, some suffering is the result of sin, especially on a corporate scale. As part of the human race, living in relationship with other humans, both those living and those preceding us, we suffer because we are part of a fallen world. And it is also true that certain kinds of misbehavior may well lead to certain kinds of suffering (e.g., smoking cigarettes and increased vulnerability to particular health problems). But we cannot look at the suffering of an individual and expect always to find an identifiable sin which has brought on this specific problem. Life is not that simple. Our concept of how justice ought to work in this world will often be frustrated by reality. Innocent people do suffer. Often, they suffer more than those who do not appear to be so innocent.

Job is a classic example of the innocent sufferer. His story challenges any view which pretends to know more about why humans suffer than experience is able to confirm. The mere acknowledgment that there is such a thing as innocent suffering is a great word of comfort to many who, as if suffering is not enough, have added to their burden the belief that somehow their suffering was their own fault.

If Job is not innocent, then no one is. God himself declared him so. In fact, if anything, Job is singled out for suffering because of his virtue, not because of his sin.

2. Who is Satan and how does he relate to God?

Satan is a strange figure. What is he doing up there in heaven? Why does God let him get away with it? What kind of control does God have over Satan? To be sure, our story of Job tells us that God puts limits on Satan's activity. Perhaps that is supposed to bring us some comfort. But look how far Satan is allowed to go. Why should God allow *any* harm to come to Job? Should God not protect human beings from the likes of Satan rather than give permission to let the aggravation go ahead?

The book of Job is one of the few places in the Old Testament where Satan appears as a heavenly being. The only other examples are in 1 Chron.

21:1 and Zech. 3:1-2. In earlier Old Testament stories, the Hebrew word *satan* is used to represent human adversaries, as in 1 Kings 11:14,23,25. The word *satan* is not used to describe the snake in the story of the fall in Genesis 3, though later theologians have certainly made connections between the snake and the Satan. Some Old Testament passages picture nonhuman forces hostile to God in the form of sea monsters whom God has slain and put under his dominion, e.g., Isa. 27:1; 51:9-10; Job 7:12; 26:12.

There seems to be a development in the thinking of the Hebrews, perhaps influenced by their Persian captors, toward a mild form of dualism (i.e., the existence of both hostile and friendly heavenly beings) by the postexilic period (after 538 B.C.E.). By that time some biblical writers dared to be more specific in personifying cosmic evil forces hostile to God. It was unreasonable to blame human beings for all the evil in the world. And some events were so horrible that you would not ascribe them to God. So it became common to speak of a demonic force (separate from and hostile toward both God and humans) responsible for at least some of the woes of the world.

The book of Job seems to come from a time (the postexilic period) when the religious community is beginning to speak of Satan as such a supernatural being. (The whole matter, however, becomes much more complicated if Chaps. 1–2 represent an older story.) The writer does not want to say too much or give too much power to Satan. God is still God and has the final authority. Satan cannot do anything without getting God's permission. God sets limits. The poet is well aware of the difficulties of talking about a being like Satan. How do you balance God's will and intention for us with the freedom given to Satan to harass us? If there is a cosmic evil force, like the devil or Satan, which is responsible for some of the evil of the world, then how does that harmonize with the idea of a God who has all things under control?

The first two chapters of Job introduce the idea of a Satan but still leave the final say with God. Perhaps that is as good a way to understand it as any.

3. Is this story harmful to our image of God?

Many readers of the book of Job are troubled by the way God is portrayed in this biblical book. Through most of the book, God does not speak, though God is addressed by Job and often mentioned by Job and the counselors. In the few places where God appears in the story, God says and does things that make us uncomfortable. God seems too willing to let Satan have his way. Though Job had just been hailed as one of the greatest human beings who ever lived, God rather casually permits this faithful and good man to be exposed to all sorts of terrible things. That seems to be a rather cruel and compassionless way to treat your most valued servant.

Two impulses are common among the readers of Job. On the one hand, there are those who are quick to defend God, to put the best possible construction on all God's words and actions, to find some ways to explain away the dark side of God, the arbitrariness, the cruelty, the vulnerability to Satan's arguments. Most of us who speak from within the church tend to fall in this category.

On the other hand, the way God is portrayed in the prolog of Job brings out a response of anger in other readers. Such a reaction is common among those outside the faith and they might even cite this example as one of the reasons why they don't believe in God anymore. Those within the church who have difficulty harmonizing the God of Job with the God they know from other parts of Scripture tend to dismiss this view of God as incomplete and insist that it must be balanced by other images, particularly those which come to us through the death and resurrection of Jesus.

When God made his wager with Satan, did God know how it would come out? The question of the foreknowledge of God is an important one in determining how we understand what God was doing in these first two chapters. If God knew for certain that Job would hold fast, then God's choice of Job would be an honor, an affirmation of God's trust. God is so sure that Job will not change, even in adversity, that he is willing to put his own reputation on the line in a wager with Satan. Job is the chosen human being through whom God puts down Satan's arguments once and for all.[12]

But did God really know how it would all turn out? Are there some doubts even in the mind of God which were stirred when Satan raised the point about Job's motivation? The text is not clear about what is going on inside God's own mind. Even God has no guarantee that God's people will always be obedient and faithful in the face of temptations and trials. The biblical story provides many examples of those who did not always live up to God's expectations for them. Some interpreters of these chapters have put the emphasis on God's desire to be loved and served unconditionally, not only because of rewards or punishments that God might bring. The only way that God can know for sure whether Job loves him with a disinterested love is to take away all his wonderful gifts and then see what happens. Like a beautiful woman or wealthy man who never knows if love is given only for selfish reasons, God does not know if Job loves God without ulterior motive until Satan is allowed to carry out the test.[13]

Who is being tested and for what purpose? For whose benefit is Job allowed to suffer? If God is already certain that Job will stand firm, then it seems that the purpose of Job's suffering is to make a point to Satan, or any others who have bought his cynical belief that there is no such thing as disinterested love of God.

If God has serious doubts about how Job will respond to adversity, then it is possible that Job is allowed to suffer in order to prove something to God himself.

There is still a third possibility. Perhaps the suffering is to make a point to Job because Job needs to know that God is still present in times of suffering as well as in times of prosperity and good health.

However one answers these questions, there will be difficulties in one's image of God. On the one hand, we have a God who knows and controls everything, but is willing to expose a faithful servant to great pain for the sake of making a point. On the other hand, we have a God who is somewhat more like us, vulnerable to doubts, uncertain how events will work out, in need of love given freely by his own creatures. Some people are more comfortable with a God who has power, even though compassion is slighted. Others feel less offended and more friendly toward a God who has great compassion and love for us but whose power is conditioned by our human response.

4. Is submission always the appropriate response to adversity?

We religious people are usually relieved when a sufferer responds to personal disasters the way that Job did in the prolog. After each stage in Satan's attack, Job girds up his loins, keeps a stiff upper lip, and insists that whatever God does is OK. It is much easier to deal with those who handle trouble this way than to be confronted with sufferers who respond with anger (toward God and humans), hard questions about God's power or goodness, or even disbelief. In many people's minds, the Job of Chaps. 1–2 has become the model of the way a pious person should react when misery comes. People who have never read the book of Job have an idea about the kind of person Job was—patient, stoic, unbending, faithful to the end, never saying an unkind word about God. The phrase "patient as Job" has become a common saying in our conversation. This is the picture of Job which has prevailed in the tradition of the church throughout the centuries.

Should a religious person always submit to reality without fighting back or complaining? Is there no room for lament? Is it not proper at times even to question God? We certainly do not have the whole story of Job if we stop with the first two chapters, though that is apparently what has happened in the minds of many people. The silent and submissive Job of the prolog acts much differently throughout most of the book, beginning already in Chap. 3. Is this to be explained merely by postulating different authors for the prolog and the poetic sections of the book? Though there may be truth to that theory, more needs to be said. Conceivably, the same person who stifles the lament at one stage may find it impossible to keep quiet at a later stage. Resignation, giving up, and turning it all over to God may be highly desirable as a way of dealing with suffering. Some people can move directly to that response. Most persons, however, need a process of lamenting, of expressing their pain and anger and frustration, before they are ready to accept the inevitable with some dignity and grace. Job, it seems to me, needed time to lament. In Chaps. 1–2 he was putting on a good front. Maybe he was saying what he thought he should say. Perhaps he even thought he could avoid the process of lament. But when his friends showed through their presence, weeping and sitting with him for seven days, that they wanted to understand what was happening to him, he dared to open up with a lament (Chap. 3). Very quickly, he found that they liked him better as a silent sufferer than as a complaining one.

Many who have tried to follow the model of Job in Chaps. 1–2 have been disappointed in themselves and have felt guilty because their own response to suffering has been less noble. People like that could be helped by walking with Job beyond the prolog and into the rest of the book.

5. Does God hurt others to affect us?

The first assault on Job by Satan was directed against his property and his family. Only in the second stage was Job's own physical person subject to attack. The nature of Job's suffering in the first stage raises a significant question. "Does God hurt others to bring about some effect in my life?" It does seem a bit self-centered to interpret another person's suffering as if its purpose is to bring about a change in me, teach me a lesson, or punish me. Job is presented to us as the sufferer. The story is about him, not about his children. One of the ways in which he suffers is by the loss of his servants and, especially, his children. Now it is true that those losses would have a terrible effect on Job. But what about the servants and the children? It may be tough on Job to grieve their death, but (since they are the ones who are dead) it would not seem inappropriate to suggest that it was even harder on them. Are they not also persons for whom God cares? If God has some intention in mind for Job, what plan does God have for those who have even given up their life in the process of working out that purpose?

One could find other places in the Bible where the death of one is seen as the result of the sin of another, e.g., the death of the first child of David and Bathsheba as a consequence of David's sins of adultery and murder (2 Sam. 12:14). One often hears religious people saying things like this. A wife tries to find meaning for her life in the death of her husband, parents search for some positive explanation for the chronic illness of their daughter, a father interprets his son's failures as judgment on himself (not on his son). Taken to excess, it is as if even the worst things that can happen to those close to us are to be understood primarily with regard to the effect they are meant to have on us. A pastoral counselor often hears such things. The first chapter of Job provides us an example of a biblical text that has influenced the way people interpret in intensely personal ways the disasters that happen to their loved ones.

3

The First Cycle of Speeches (Job 3-14)

Job is the first to break the silence that had lasted for a week. The counselors had not preached to Job about his misfortunes. They had not yet interpreted his troubles for him. It was not they who spoke first, but Job. And when he spoke it was words of lament and woe, not the stoic, submissive, patient, and pious sayings of Chaps. 1–2.

Job's Opening Lament (Chapter 3)

"Let the day of my birth be cursed" (3:1-10)

Job is not the only biblical character to sing such a mournful refrain. Jeremiah, too, cursed the day of his birth in what is probably the most poignant of his confessions (Jer. 20:14-18). The writer of the book of Job probably knew the passage from Jeremiah.[14]

The Hebrew word for "curse" in v. 1 is a common word for "curse" (*qll*), and not the euphemism which we noted in Chaps. 1–2. Job had refrained from cursing God after each level of persecution brought on by the Satan. He still stops short of cursing God in Chap. 3. He wonders why he was born into a life that has brought so much misery and he wonders why death does not come more quickly to remove him from his painful existence. But he does not curse, blame, renounce, or blaspheme God. Not yet, anyway.

We are accustomed to celebrating birthdays in our families. We honor and relish the day on which a loved one came into the world, the beginning of a life that has touched ours and for which we are thankful. Job's cry is a bitter irony, a perverse upside-down version of "Happy Birthday to Me." Instead of celebrating the day which marks the beginning of one's life, Job has descended to the depth of deploring that day and that life. It would be better never to have been born, never to have emerged from the womb, than to live in such constant trouble.

"At least there is rest in death" (3:11-19)

Death doesn't look so bad to Job. For most human beings, death is an enemy, the threatened end to our existence, the inevitable which we seek to block from our consciousness as if to ignore it will keep it from touching us. But sometimes life is so bad that death can begin to look like a friend, a way out, an escape. Though certainly an unknown, it cannot be worse than what is known. If Job had died at birth or as an infant, then he would now be resting and he would have avoided all his past and present miseries. He would be in the same situation as all those who have already lived and have now died, whether they be kings or slaves. Death is the great equalizer. A miserable person like Job is no worse off in death than the mightiest of princes. Further, in death, the wicked cannot do their dirty work anymore, the weary get rest, and the slaves are finally free from their masters. "Death may not be so bad after all," says Job.

When friends and acquaintances begin to talk like this, we become alarmed. When death starts to look more appealing than life, we decide it's time to call for professional help. Job had reached that point.

"Why doesn't the relief of death come?" (3:20-26)

"Why doesn't God take him?" The old man has had a good life. But now his wife is gone. His friends, too, have died ahead of him. His mind is only occasionally in contact with the present world. He can barely see and hardly hear. His pain seems to be almost constant. But his heart is strong and he won't die. Why does God let him stay alive? Why does God hedge him in to protect him from death when it seems apparent that this is a time when death would be a relief, a sweet escape from what is left of this life and its pain and decay?

So thought Job. He is consumed by dread. He has no peace, no rest, no quiet. Why cannot he die and get it all over with? We know from the prolog that God had stipulated that Satan was not to kill him (2:6). Strangely, that word of restraint on the part of God has now become an extra burden to Job, who, at least at this point in his journey, wonders if death would not be preferable to this.

Eliphaz (Chapters 4–5)

Eliphaz is the first to respond to this outburst from Job. What should he say? His good friend has been uttering some awful things. He is genuinely troubled by what he hears. He wishes he knew how to move Job out of this terrible mood that he is in. Eliphaz is no novice at this. He has been around. He knows a few things about religion. He has thought about suffering and where it comes from and why it hits some people and not others. Job is admittedly a tough case. It is hard to figure why such a fine man should have to go through all this. And now Job, who used to be so upbeat all the time, is so depressed that it sounds as though he wants to give up and die.

Someone must speak. Job has said some things which call for a response. Eliphaz steps forward to see what he can do. He draws on the resources of his religious tradition and his own experience. He, as it turns out, is the wisest of the three counselors, and he is at his best in his first attempt in Chaps. 4 and 5.

"Practice what you preach" (4:1-5)

Eliphaz begins with deference. He wishes not to offend Job, but he cannot keep silent any longer. As hard as he tries to be gentle and sensitive to Job's condition, the first words from Eliphaz come across as a mild rebuke. "Job, you used to be a counselor yourself. You have taught and supported many people when they were in distress not unlike your own. But now that you are sitting in the hot seat yourself, you are impatient and dismayed." If only Job could think on those words which he himself used to speak to others in their times of trouble.

To whom does the doctor go when sick? To whom does the minister go when faith has deserted him? Where does one go for answers when one already knows the answers but they don't make sense anymore? The one who is there to help others should be better able to handle trouble than others. How can the bearer of good news be depressed? "Don't you believe that message you've been preaching all these years?" We can understand doubt and depression in some people, but others should know better. A person like Job is particularly vulnerable to a comment like this one from Eliphaz. Job is not even allowed the doubts of an ordinary human being. Though he may think he is being helpful, Eliphaz has already wounded Job by hitting a very sensitive spot.

"The doctrine of retribution works" (4:6-11)

"The doctrine of retribution works. You can count on that, Job." Eliphaz tells Job that this should be a word of encouragement to him. Since Job has been a pious man and a moral man, he should take hope from that (v. 6). Since God will eventually see that the good are rewarded in this life, then Job should have a good life to look forward to, even though he is having a little difficulty right now. At this point in the conversation, Eliphaz agrees that Job is a good man and therefore can expect the present trouble to pass.

Eliphaz goes on (vv. 7-9) to articulate clearly his belief in the doctrine of retribution. He asks the question whether anyone who was innocent has ever perished or been cut off. The question seems to imply that the answer would be "No; I can't think of any case where that has happened." Eliphaz probably has come to these beliefs on the basis of his own religious tradition but he also claims that he has concluded this to be true from his personal observations of life (v. 8a). The innocent are never cut off and "those who sow trouble reap the same" (v. 8b).

How could Eliphaz say this? Had he really never met any innocent persons who were suffering much more than they deserved? Had he never heard of some wicked tormentor of the poor who had lived to a happy and healthy and wealthy old age without ever shedding a tear of remorse? If he is looking for that single case that would blow his theory out of the water, what about Job himself? When Eliphaz says to Job, "Who that was innocent ever perished?" Job could well have answered, "What about me?"

Though the words do not sound so harsh on the surface, we can imagine the effect they were beginning to have on Job, the innocent sufferer. "If my friend Eliphaz really believes that no one who is innocent has ever been brought to the point of perishing, then what does he think about me?" When Eliphaz finishes talking, Job will direct some hard words against his counselors. We must look carefully at what Eliphaz is saying to see why Job becomes so angry.

"I had a revelation—all are sinners" (4:12-21)

Eliphaz is an interesting character. All of a sudden he changes his approach and recounts a strange religious experience which he has had. He does not say when it happened (could it have come during those long seven days and seven nights sitting in silence with Job trying to figure out what to say when someone would finally break the ice?). His description of a vision in the night has an eerie quality—dread and shaking bones and hair standing on end and a ghostly apparition (vv. 12-16). There are not many episodes quite like this recorded in the Bible. We have already formed an image of what kind of person Eliphaz is—a teacher of religion, respected, learned, a student of human life, and a counselor to those in trouble. And now we find another side to his personality. He is a "charismatic." He has religious experiences which most people don't have. So Eliphaz speaks not only from the authority of the religious teachings that he has learned and his personal observations. He also claims a special revelation.

And what is the content of this word that comes in such a strange way? After the suspenseful buildup, what is this great religious insight to share with Job? "All human beings are sinners." No mere mortal can be righteous or pure before the Creator (v. 17). Eliphaz has obviously been struggling with reconciling his belief in the predictability of divine retribution with the apparent innocence of Job. It is cases like Job's which are hard to handle. But then comes the revelation. All human beings are sinners, even good people like Job. Therefore, anyone is eligible for suffering because no one is perfect. If you look hard enough, you can find sin in even the sweetest old lady or kindest old man. Therefore, the doctrine of retribution is right after all. We all deserve any suffering that comes to us. The wonder is that we are not all suffering because, in God's eyes, we all deserve it. There is no such thing as innocent suffering because there is no such thing as an innocent human being. This theme of the huge gap between the righteousness of God and the frailty of humans is expanded in the last few verses of the chapter (vv. 18-21).

What Eliphaz says is no doubt true. But it could hardly have been much of a comfort to poor Job. Are there no distinctions to make? Job is still left with the question, "If we are all sinners, then why are we not all suffering? Why me and not someone else?" On a comparative scale, Job is still more deserving of a good life and less in need of punishment than almost any other human being. (Remember God's boasting about him.) Further, this line of argument by Eliphaz opens the door to a relentless probing into the life of Job to try to locate (since we now grant that Job is a sinner) the specific sin which is lurking under the surface and must be uncovered and repented before health can return. The advocate of the doctrine of retribution is pushed by the logic of his or her position to blame the sufferer for getting into such a fix. The other counselors will follow Eliphaz in this, and Job will not like it.

"Humans bring trouble on themselves" (5:1-7)

This is a very difficult passage to understand. There are several problems with the text, especially in vv. 3 and 5, and many suggestions have been made to try to clarify the meaning.[15] For some reason, Eliphaz tells Job that it will do no good to appeal to one of the angels for answers to his questions (v. 1).

Job had not suggested that, though later in the book he will express his wish for a mediator between God and himself. Eliphaz goes on to talk about the misfortunes that befall fools and the families of fools (vv. 2-5). Perhaps there is some intimation that this applies to Job and his deceased sons. Finally, in vv. 6-7, Eliphaz seems to be saying that trouble does not come without good reason ("For affliction does not come from the dust, nor does trouble sprout from the ground"). Human beings bring their trouble on themselves. It is not just bad luck or blind fate. This is consistent with what Eliphaz has been saying and, in line with that, a better translation than "but man is born to trouble" (v. 7a, RSV) would be "man brings trouble on himself" (as in TEV and JB).[16]

"Have faith—like me" (5:8-16)

Eliphaz now dares to tell Job what he would do if he were in Job's shoes (v. 8). "If I were you I would put my trust in God." Good advice. Put your trust in God. Have faith. But Eliphaz does not *really* know what he would do if he were subject to the same trials as Job. "Lead us not into temptation," we say in the Lord's Prayer (unless we are now saying, "Save us from the time of trial"). We do not know how much we can take before our faith is forced to the breaking point and our doubts harden into disbelief. Beware the counselor who is bold enough to say, "If I were you, this is what I would do."

Eliphaz goes on to support his statement about committing oneself to God by supplying a beautiful expression of confidence in God's providence (vv. 9-16). God does remarkable things which we cannot even begin to list, but Eliphaz goes on to mention a few—the giving of rain, lifting the lowly and bringing the mighty down to size, giving hope and justice to the poor. This is a typical biblical reference to the work of God in the world, common in many psalms and elsewhere (e.g., Hannah's song in 1 Sam. 2:1-10 and the Magnificat in Luke 1:46-55). Job should put his trust in God who has acted like this in the past and can be trusted to continue. Many have found great comfort in words like these from Eliphaz. But that was not the effect which they worked in Job.

"Chastisement is good for you" (5:17-27)

Eliphaz is not a rigid, doctrinaire person. He is struggling to help Job find some explanation which will ease the burden of his suffering. He is particularly interested in finding an interpretation of Job's suffering which will protect his image of a God who is good and who is also just. He is finding that it is very hard to minimize God's part in the origin of suffering without putting the blame on the sufferer. The observation that all human beings are less than righteous before God is an effort to make sense of God's justice without being too hard on Job. In 5:17-27, Eliphaz tries another approach. Job's suffering may not be punishment but rather is for the purpose of education or correction. The one whom God reproves and chastens should be happy to be singled out for such attention and should submit to that discipline and attempt to learn what God intends to teach through the suffering (5:17).

The rest of this chapter contains some very nice words from Eliphaz about God's presence with us even in times of danger and suffering. Though God may test us for a time, we have the promise that we will never be pushed beyond what we will be able to endure (vv. 18-22). One is reminded of other biblical passages (several in New Testament epistles) that say almost the same thing that Eliphaz is saying to Job. "No temptation has overtaken you that is not common to man. God is faithful, and he will not let you be tempted beyond your strength, but with the temptation will also provide the way of escape, that you may be able to endure it" (1 Cor. 10:13). "My son, do not despise the Lord's discipline or be weary of his reproof, for the Lord reproves him whom he loves, as a father the son in whom he delights" (Prov. 3:11-12, quoted in Heb. 12:5-6). Later in the book of Job, Elihu will follow this same train of thought.

Here Eliphaz provides one of the most common ways of understanding suffering. It is good for us. It can help us become better persons. "Thanks, God, I needed that." If we will be submissive toward God and take his chastening to heart, our lives after the suffering is over will be even better than before (5:23-26). Eliphaz is in good company. Many a preacher and pastoral counselor has spoken words of intended comfort that are virtually identical to those spoken by Job's first comforter. Sometimes people have been greatly helped by such words. Others, like Job, have responded to such pious phrases with anger. Though less direct than the retribution doctrine, this view of suffering has a condemning tone because it implies that the sufferer has flaws that are serious enough to require such drastic means of correction.

Eliphaz closes his speech with a rather pompous word of certainty. He has come to his conclusions after long study and observation of the world. Therefore, Job should accept what has been said (5:27). Eliphaz has given good advice. We can find passages elsewhere in Scripture that support the points which he has made. And yet, Job resists. Words that sound like comfort in some situations sound like criticism and condemnation to Job. He will not take the insinuations and subtle negative judgments of his character without an argument. And so Job responds.

Job Responds (Chapters 6–7)

"My words are rash, but for good reason" (6:1-7)

How can you measure someone else's suffering? Job begins by being somewhat apologetic about his rash words (v. 3), but his friends must try to realize how severely he has been provoked. From their positions of health and security they find it difficult to empathize with his experience. He would not be speaking so wildly if there were not good cause. Verses 5-7 are meant to reinforce this point, though the precise meaning of the Hebrew is impossible to determine.

Job's words in v. 4 leap out at us because of what they say about Job's understanding of God's part in his present miseries. He believes that God has shot him with poisonous arrows. He accuses God of causing his suffering. This is a logical conclusion from Job's presupposition that God is powerful and can do whatever God wants in the world. If Job had some reason why God would do such a thing to him, then he could continue to believe in the justice of God. But as he looks at the innocence of his own life and the wicked people in the world who continue to prosper, Job begins to wonder about God's goodness and fairness. This is an important turning point in Job's response to his suffering. In the prolog, Job did not yet question why God brought these calamities on him. In his lament (Chap. 3), Job did not directly accuse God of being unfair. In this passage, Job has not yet brought that charge against God, but he is getting mighty close.

"Let me die now for I have no hope" (6:8-13)

Job again expresses the desire to die. If only God would hear his prayer and blot him out. (We are reminded of his longing for death in Chap. 3.) So far Job has not "denied the words of the Holy One" (6:10b). But he is not sure how much more he can take (vv. 11-12). Perhaps he has already been frightened by the thought that God has poisoned him (6:4) and he is concerned that if this suffering goes on too long he will not be able to control himself anymore. He may even turn against God in anger for all that has happened. In spite of Eliphaz's assurance that God will not push him beyond the breaking point, he is not so sure. Better to die now and be done with it than to see even his relationship with God destroyed.

Job feels that it is hopeless. He will never get better. He has no inner resources on which to draw (v. 13a), his faith in a good God is wavering, and, after the speech by Eliphaz, he now realizes that there will be no help from any human source ("and any resource is driven from me," v. 13b).

"You are terrible counselors" (6:14-30)

Suddenly there is an escalation in the rhetoric. Eliphaz had spoken with deference, searching for the right words to say, drawing on the religious teachings of the day as well as his personal experience. Many scholars have been a little shocked by the sharpness of Job's response to Eliphaz. They think Job is the one who takes the lead in the deterioration of the relationship between the counselors and the suffering Job. Why should Job respond in such a critical way to the good intentions of his friend? We have already noted the hint of accusation and blame that lies close to the surface in all that Eliphaz has said. It should not be a complete surprise that Job responds as he does.

Job says that he especially needs kindness right now, but his friends have not given it to him.[17] Like streams that go dry after the rain, they disappear when things get hot (vv. 15-17). They have taken a close look at Job's calamity and are afraid (v. 21b). Fear is not an uncommon emotion when we are called upon to visit someone like Job. What are we going to say? We want to speak a word that will be helpful. We wish we had the power to make the pain go away. We wonder how we will respond to the hard "Why?" questions. We know we have no good answer and we are afraid that we will look stupid or helpless. We are even afraid that our own faith might suffer as we are forced to agonize with another about the meaning of their suffering. We don't have any easy answers, any miracle solution, any power to change things.

Job tells them that he knows that. He knows the limitations of his counselors. They cannot make his pain go away. He is not asking them to do that (vv. 22-23) and therefore they should not be afraid or embarrassed because they feel so helpless in the presence of his suffering. They have tried too hard to make sense out of his suffering, to explain what they cannot know, and in so doing they have taken the direction of condemning Job.

Job feels their reproof. He wants to argue about his integrity (6:28-30). If there is some sin that they know about, he wants to hear what it is (6:24). If their theories are more than empty abstractions, they should be specific and not hide behind vague generalities and sly innuendos.

In v. 26, Job again admits that his words are rash (as in 6:3) and he asks his friends not to dwell too much on the content of his words but to reach out to him at a deeper level. "Do you think that you can reprove words, when the speech of a despairing man is wind?" Do not argue with the words of a desperate man or woman. When persons are hurting badly enough, they will say things that would never be uttered in the calm of a more pleasant time. A sufferer does not want to argue over words that are emotional responses to great tribulation as if they were carefully defined and well balanced intellectual propositions about the presence of evil in the world. The counselor should know enough to recognize which is which and to respond accordingly. Job, in the form of a lament, cries for help and understanding—but his friends want to argue theology. Job and his counselors are working on two different levels. He attempts to tell them how they have missed the point of his outburst, but his criticism of them only confirms them in their efforts to find the hidden cause of his suffering, the defect which needs correction, the sin that has been masked by the pious exterior. The nasty way he talks to them will make it all the more clear that he is not as good a person as they had thought.

"My life is miserable" (7:1-6)

Job returns to the lament. Life is tough. Human beings are like slaves, forced to work hard, with little to hope for except an occasional respite in the shade when the day's work is done (vv. 1-2). There is little meaning to a life filled with "months of emptiness" and "nights of misery" (v. 3). Nights have become times of fitful tossing rather than the periods of rest which they should be (v. 4). Verse 5 is one of the few places where Job describes his physical affliction.

Job says that his days are passing by swiftly and without hope (v. 6). Earlier, Job had reflected that death would be better than such a terrible life. Here Job is lamenting the fact that life, terrible though it may be, passes by too quickly. Many sufferers have noted, like Job, that the days and nights seem endless, and they wonder how they can possibly make it from one day to the next. At the same time, life slips away and death approaches at an ever-accelerating speed. How can a night seem so long and a lifetime so short?

"God, stop picking on me!" (7:7-21)

Now Job addresses God directly. Up to this time, Job has either been speaking to his counselors or talking indirectly to God, e.g., "If only God would grant my desire and crush me" (as in 6:8-9). But now Job cannot restrain himself. He must speak out of his anguish (7:11). As he approaches God, Job reminds God that his life is short and almost over and he will soon disappear before God's eyes (7:7-8). Those who die and go to Sheol will never return and will soon be forgotten even by those who know them best (7:9-10). Job seems to be playing on God's sympathy, with the hint that if God does not act soon, Job will be dead and gone and it will be too late.

"Leave me alone, God." That is the outcry from Job in these next few verses. "Get off my back, God. I am no threat to you." In v. 12, Job refers to the primordial sea monster which God defeated when he first created order out of chaos. If Job were such a cosmic force in hostile competition with God, then he would warrant such constant attention. But he is only a human being, no danger to God Almighty. God will not leave Job alone—tormenting him even in his dreams so that he is driven to preferring death to life (vv. 13-15). There is no relief, no place to hide, no letup in God's constant meddling in the lives of human beings. Verses 17-19 are a cruel mockery of Psalm 8 ("What is man that thou art mindful of him?" Ps. 8:4a).

Is it better to have a God who is always hanging over your shoulder, aware of everything that you do, always making a judgment whether you've "been naughty or nice," or would it be better to have a God who took somewhat less interest in human beings and was not so preoccupied with keeping a constant watch on their behavior? Is the omnipresence of God good or bad? Does Job's sin hurt God (v. 20)? Why has God decided to focus so much attention on Job? Job does not know the story of what went on in heaven between Satan and God. If he knew that, Job, if anything, might have asked this question with even more vehemence.

Job closes with a desperate cry for God to forgive whatever sin he may have committed and to stop this punishment (v. 21a). Though he often talks as if he is innocent, Job is not claiming to be without sin. There may be sins of which he is not even aware. He only wants to be treated fairly compared to the way other people are treated.

Job finishes his speech with the mournful theme with which this section began. If God doesn't act soon, Job will be dead, and God will look for him and he will be gone (21b). His thinking here is like that of a child who has just been punished by a parent and cries out in anguish, "You will miss me when I'm gone."

Bildad (Chapter 8)

Next in line is Bildad. The tone of the discussion is on its way downhill. We have already seen the high point in the presentations by the counselors in the first speech of Eliphaz. Job's words in Chaps. 6–7 were not received well by Bildad. He is quick to come to God's defense. And he is much more direct and forceful than Eliphaz in his application of the doctrine of retribution to the life of Job.

"How dare you imply God is not just!" (8:1-7)

Bildad goes right after Job, accusing him of speaking "windy" words (v. 2). Job himself had admitted that "the speech of a despairing man is wind" (6:26b). Nevertheless, Bildad treats Job's words as if they are a great threat to the prevailing doctrine of God and how God works in the world. Again, Bildad makes the mistake of taking the words of a lament and arguing with the sufferer instead of listening to the pain. When a sufferer cries out, "My God, why have you forsaken me? Why are you hiding from me?" we should hear the loneliness of one who feels deserted by God and not argue that "Your understanding of God is wrong because God is always present and never forsakes or hides from us." When Job begins to raise serious questions about God's justice, Bildad feels compelled to defend the doctrine that God is just (v. 3) rather than to listen to the pain that has driven Job to such a position.

In order to demonstrate the truth of his position, Bildad dares to point to a recent event in Job's life. He has the audacity to interpret why Job's children were killed. They must have done something to deserve what happened to them because God is just and whatever evil comes to us must have a reason (v. 4). What a cruel and heartless thing to say to the man who has lost all of his offspring in one horrendous calamity! How does Bildad know? Who gave him such insights that he can explain why Job's children died? Even if it were true (which it isn't, as we know from Chap. 1), Bildad's accusing way of dealing with Job would be a horrible example of how to comfort a sufferer. Bildad is obviously more concerned with defending doctrine than helping Job.

Bildad goes on, in self-righteous arrogance, to tell Job that if he will seek God and make himself pure, then God will reward him with blessings that will overshadow even his former prosperity (vv. 5-7). It is like telling an innocent man to plead guilty in order to get off with a light sentence. Job has too much integrity to play that game. If Job became angry after Eliphaz spoke, we can imagine what his response will be after Bildad.

"Learn from your ancestors" (8:8-10)

Bildad reminds Job of the value of the teachings passed on to us throughout the centuries by teachers who have lived through the problems of life and have left us the benefit of their insights. We live but a short time and must depend on those who went before us for wisdom and understanding. Each generation can build on the knowledge of the previous generations. We do not need to reinvent the wheel.

If our own experience seems to contradict what we have been taught, we should be hesitant to throw out the wisdom of the ages on the basis of our limited perspective. Truth that has lasted for centuries cannot be dismissed casually as if the experience of one individual can offset what has been acceptable teaching by a large consensus over a long period of time. This is particularly true for teaching which has hardened into sacred doctrine.

What do we do when our experience makes ancient doctrine seem untrue? Is it possible that one person might be right in the face of centuries of tradition?

Should we retreat in submission to the traditional teaching, not daring to risk the vulnerability of being in opposition to the great teachers of the past? That is the dilemma in which Job finds himself. Bildad is, of course, referring to the doctrine of retribution when he tells Job to look at the wisdom of the fathers. God is just and works in the world to punish the wicked and reward the faithful. Job is told to quit protesting and accept that truth, even though, from his limited vision, he is having trouble seeing how it works in his own life. Don't doubt God's justice merely on the basis of what has happened to you. Job, as we have said, still believes in the doctrine of retribution. He, like Bildad, has learned from those teachers who went before. As Job sees it, the problem is that God is not operating according to the rules.

"God's justice is sure for wicked and innocent alike" (8:11-22)

Bildad closes his discourse with some observations about the certainty of God's justice. There are observable cause-and-effect relationships between what people do and what happens to them. As plants without water will wither and die (vv. 11-12), so will perish "the hope of the godless man" (v. 13). It is inevitable. Though the wicked person may appear to prosper for a time, there is no hope without God's support (vv. 14-19), and God will not give help to the evildoer (v. 20b). The other side of God's justice is the assurance that "God will not reject a blameless man" (v. 20a). Bildad closes with some words of reassurance for Job, telling him that he again will be able to laugh and his enemies will be appropriately punished (vv. 21-22).

Once more the case has been made for the doctrine of retribution. The world makes sense. Learn from the teachings of your ancestors. Godlessness will lead to trouble. God will never abandon those who are faithful to him, so have hope (assuming you are one who is faithful). There is much truth in what Bildad says, as a general description of the world. Sin may lead to suffering. But a particular example of suffering may not be the result of sin. It may have some other cause, or no reasonable explanation at all. Bildad's most flagrant error is to be specific in making a connection between the death of Job's children and some sin on their part. He claims to know too much, and turns out to be dead wrong.

Job's Response (Chapters 9–10)

"God does what he wants with the world" (9:1-13)

Job responds to Eliphaz as well as Bildad. Some have suggested that v. 2 is actually a reply to Eliphaz's contention that no human being can be righteous before God (4:17). Later in Chap. 9, Job argues against claims made by both Eliphaz and Bildad that God's actions are always just.

How can a human being argue against God (v. 3)? Even if you thought that God was not just, what recourse would you have? No matter what you say, God could come up with more questions (which a human being could never be able to answer) that would further confuse the issue. This is, in fact, what God does when he finally confronts Job in Chap. 38. There are other similarities between this chapter and God's speeches, as Job goes on to talk about God's power and control over his creation (vv. 5-13). God can do what God wants with the world without answering to anyone. No human being can play in that league. If you don't like the way God has written the rules or administers them, do you dare stand up to protest? No one could expect to succeed at defying God (v. 4b).

In this chapter Job has anticipated what will in fact happen in his confrontation with God in Chaps. 38–41. At that point, after daring to challenge God, Job will be overwhelmed by many questions which highlight his inability to understand all the mysteries of the universe. God's power and control of the world will be recited to Job by God, just as Job himself had said God would do.

"God is both prosecuting attorney and judge" (9:14-19)

Job continues to use courtroom imagery to describe his present relationship with God. He stands convicted, as demonstrated by the suffering with which he is afflicted. Somehow he must convince God that he is really innocent. But how can he do that? The system is working against him. How can he get a fair hearing from the one who is his accuser (v. 15b)?[18] Job believes that God has brought his troubles upon him (vv. 17-18). Therefore, God is not impartial toward Job. A judge is supposed to approach a case with an open mind, but God has already decided about Job. So God acts as both prosecuting attorney and judge. And there is no way to bring God into account, no supreme court to whom an appeal can be made, no way to force God to listen to the case (vv. 16, 19).

Job's close and loving relationship with God has come to this. God is the accuser. God is unfair. It is all so cold and mechanistic and lacking in compassion. It is difficult to come to God for comfort in a time of great distress when you are convinced that God is the one who is causing all your trouble—and for no good reason.

"God is not just" (9:20-24)

Job has been working up to this point. Eliphaz says there has never been an innocent person who has perished (4:7) and Bildad is convinced that God will never abandon the good person or give aid to the evildoer (8:20). Job has been struggling with these words of his counselors. Gradually, the awful thought has been taking shape in Job's mind that God is not just, that good people suffer more than they deserve and wicked people are not brought to judgment. He sees himself as the prime example of the innocent sufferer (vv. 20-21). He finally comes right out and says it. There are no distinctions—God destroys both the blameless and the wicked (v. 22). God laughs at the death of the innocent (v. 23). God has given the world to wicked people and has blinded the judges. And if God is not to blame for the rampant injustice of the world, then who is (v. 24)?

These are hard words. God's justice is under direct attack. Eliphaz and Bildad are wrong, naive, unrealistic, simplistic. If God is really God, if God has the final say about what takes place in the world, then it follows that God is not just.

"I can never be clean" (9:25-31)

Job continues with a lament. We are far enough into the book of Job that we begin to feel the repetition. What has been said before will be said again. There will be fewer and fewer new points to make. In vv. 25-26, Job reiterates his feeling that life is slipping away from him (cf. 7:6). Job is convinced that God will continue to condemn, that there is no way that he can prove his innocence (vv. 28-31). No matter how hard he tries to clean himself, God will throw him back into a filthy pit so that even his own clothes will be repulsed by him (v. 31). (Compare this with Ps. 51:7, "Purge me with hyssop, and I shall be clean; wash me, and I shall be whiter than snow.")

"There is no umpire between us" (9:32-35)

Job again returns to the theme of the futility of taking God to court. If God were a human being, then the two of them could go to a judge to settle their dispute. But when one of the parties in a disagreement is God, there is not much chance for the second party. There is no umpire or mediator or arbiter to step between God and a human being in order to take the side of the human and argue against the way God has been executing justice. Actually, there are biblical accounts of human beings, such as Abraham and Moses, who act as mediators or intercessors on behalf of people who have been condemned by God (e.g., Gen. 18:22ff.; Num. 14:10b-20; 16:42-50). Sometimes they were even able to convince God to change the judgment. Later, Christians will use this imagery to talk about the work that Jesus does on our behalf as a mediator between sinful humans and God. Job, however, sees no mediator, human or divine, who would be able to bring God to account and bring an end to what he sees as undeserved punishment.

"Will you destroy your own creation?" (10:1-17)

Job's lament continues. He wants God to tell him why he has been treated this way. What is the charge (v. 2)? In this passage there is a return to some tenderness and nostalgia on the part of Job as he thinks about what God had meant to him in the past. God is the creator, the giver of life. Why then should God despise the very thing that God has created (v. 3)? There are some lovely thoughts in vv. 8-11 which express Job's belief in the goodness of the creation. "Thou hast granted me life and steadfast love; and thy care has preserved my spirit" (v. 12). Here Job seems to have quieted down from his previous charges of injustice on God's part. He speaks here more out of sadness and dismay than out of anger. It makes no sense that the loving God he used to know, the one who had created him in his mother's womb and who had often shown him care and love, should now want to destroy him. A loving creator should not act like that.

This passage gives us some clue about the kind of relationship that Job used to have with God before all the trouble started. Job is bewildered why the loving God of his earlier years has now turned cruel.

"Leave me alone to die in peace" (10:18-22)

Job returns to the theme of death. He is beginning to repeat himself. As in Chap. 3, he wishes he had never been born or, perhaps, had been stillborn and carried directly from womb to grave without ever having the consciousness of existence (vv. 18-19). He does not expect to live much longer. He asks God to leave him alone so that he may have some peace in the short time that he has left. Death is described as a place of gloom and darkness from which no one will return. This picture of death sounds much less appealing than the image of death as a place of rest and release from trouble in 3:13-19. Death seems less attractive to Job here than earlier in his pilgrimage.

On this mournful note Job ends his discourse.

Zophar (Chapter 11)

"Shut up, Job! You are guilty" (11:1-6)

Now the third friend, Zophar, has his turn. No doubt he has been standing by listening to all of this, waiting for an opportunity to get in his critique. The time for being subtle, wearing kid gloves, and being "Mr. Nice Guy" is over. Eliphaz had been rather restrained, though he still sounded condemnatory to Job. Bildad had suggested that Job's children deserved what they got. Zophar goes straight for the jugular. Job does not know what he is talking about. Such words cannot be allowed to stand without being challenged (vv. 2-3). Job's claims to be speaking the truth and to be pure in God's eyes (Job probably never claimed that) must be refuted (v. 4). If only God would speak to Job and straighten him out (v. 5)! (Job had also asked for that in 10:2). If that should happen, Job would find that "God exacts of you less than your guilt deserves" (v. 6).

It is said that the best defense is a good offense. If the retribution doctrine is being questioned, if an apparently good man is suffering and that raises doubts about God's justice in the world, then attack and turn the argument back on the sufferer. "The retribution doctrine does work, and you are a bigger sinner than you think." Zophar is able to be more direct than either Eliphaz or Bildad because he has heard Job speak a couple of times. He has seen Job's hostility toward God, his lack of trust in God's justice, and his exaggerated claims for innocence. By these reactions in his time of trouble, Job has begun to show what kind of person he really is. There is no reason any longer to be kind to a person who says God laughs at the calamity of the innocent and has given the world over to the hands of the wicked (9:23-24). God is just and Job is a sinner and all is right with the world.

"Stupid humans cannot know what God knows" (11:7-12)

No human being can ever fully understand God. Job is asking questions that are impossible to answer, because some mystery will always remain when humans try to figure out what God is doing. If God calls a human being to judgment, "who can hinder him?" (v. 10). God knows who is worthless and will respond to iniquity as God sees fit (v. 11). The meaning of v. 12 is not certain but the apparent intent is to show how impossible it is for a stupid man to get understanding (according to the RSV, it is about as likely an event as a wild ass giving birth to a human).

Zophar emphasizes the huge gap that lies between God and human beings. His way of fending off attacks on his own doctrinal positions is to fall back on the obvious, but not very helpful, truism that human beings cannot know everything about God. Job is already well aware of that. He himself has already said that a human being cannot contend on an equal footing with God and that God can do what God wants without having to answer to anyone. Job knows all about God's power and the difficulty of understanding why God does what he does. But Zophar uses the truth of human incapacity to understand God as a way of protecting his own position. Though he *claims* humans cannot know the mysteries of God's activity, he really believes that humans *can* know. At least he believes that he knows the reason why Job is suffering. The suffering of Job is no mystery to Zophar at all: "Know that God exacts of you less than your guilt deserves" (11:6b).

What Zophar says to Job here is not unlike what God says to Job in Chaps. 38–41. That raises some questions for us to keep in mind as we continue to look at the book of Job. If Job accepts this word from God at a later time, why cannot he accept it from Zophar now? It must have something to do with the timing (perhaps it is too early for Job to abandon his search for answers) and with the relationship between Job and the one giving the advice. It is one thing to be told by God himself that human beings are incapable of penetrating all the mysteries of life and death and God. It is another thing to be squelched by an anxious peddler of a rigid doctrine who knows that his position cannot withstand too many critical questions and so he pulls out the ultimate conversation stopper: "It's all a great mystery and therefore we cannot discuss it."

"If you repent, all will go well" (11:13-20)

Zophar assumes that Job has something of which to repent. So the way for Job's life to take a turn back to more pleasant times is to abandon wickedness and turn toward God (vv. 13-14). Zophar then recites some very pleasant, optimistic words which could be encouraging to a sinner who is doubtful whether God will forgive and life can ever be pleasant again (vv. 15-19). The problem is that Job is not such a sinner. Of what is he supposed to repent? He cannot confess to something he has not done. He has asked God to tell him where he has been wrong, but so far no one (God or his counselors) has made it clear to him where he is in the wrong.

Zophar closes with a word of warning, following his assurances that life will be wonderful after Job repents. There is no way of escape for the wicked. Death is the only hope left for them (v. 20). "Take your choice, Job. Repent and the good life will return. Persist in your wicked ways and you will be stuck in your present miserable state until death brings its own kind of relief."

Job's Response (Chapters 12–14)

Job has now heard from all three of his friends. Some patterns are developing. All of them are struggling to maintain their belief in retribution as a manifestation of God's justice. Since Job is suffering, they reason that there must be a cause, and they have become more and more straightforward in their accusations toward Job. As Job responds at the end of this first cycle, he reacts to what has been said by all three. He has some severe criticism of the way they have treated him, he turns toward God as his only hope, and he ponders the possibilities for life after death.

"I am a laughingstock" (12:1-6)

Job begins with biting sarcasm. "No doubt you are the people, and wisdom will die with you" (v. 2). Job feels that they are patronizing him. They come to him with their arrogance and pompous attitude and speak in their best preaching voice and expect him to hang on their every word as if he were a young, inexperienced, or ignorant person who had never heard such words before. Job says he is not inferior to them (v. 3). "Quit talking down your nose to me as if you know something no one else knows. All you are doing is hauling out the same old platitudes that everyone has heard and you act as though you are pronouncing a profound new word for this time and place." God protect us from preachers and pastoral counselors who talk down to us as if we did not have a brain in our head or any experience of our own.

Job has become a laughingstock, an object of laughter and derision. He used to be the person whom everyone respected, the model of a religious man. Now people wonder about him, they shy away from him, they suspect there must be a reason why he is suffering so, and they laugh at his futile efforts to defend himself and challenge God. Job recounts those good old days when he prayed and God actually answered him (v. 4). Now he is alone. Former admirers mock him. And God says nothing. Those who are well off, who have not tasted the bitterness of suffering, have contempt for misfortune (v. 5). Suffering is always a bother, especially for religious people. It does not fit neatly into our talk about a good and powerful God. Contempt for suffering can quickly become contempt for the sufferer who has dared to challenge our doctrine with his or her misery. Job's view of suffering was once like that of his friends. But now he has seen it from the other side. They are not able to understand him because they have not been there.

"God has the power to do whatever God wants" (12:7-25)

We have heard words like this from Job before (9:1-13). All creatures are in God's hands. God has made all that there is (vv. 7-10). Job then goes on to sing about the power of God to do whatever God wants with the world. Job seems to be saying that everything that happens must be God's doing, whether it be giving authority or taking it away, whether it be something that involves whole nations or individuals. God gives and God takes away (cf. 1:21). If God has decided, then no one can change it (note 12:14).

Job's problems are intensified because he believes that God controls everything that happens. Whatever happens to the world or to himself is God's doing. For Job, there is no such thing as dumb accident, blind fate, the work of evil forces, or trouble caused by other humans. Everything that happens is God's will because God controls everything. Job's suffering, then, like everything else that happens, is God's will. But why? The usual answer that suffering is a manifestation of God's will to punish the guilty is not sufficient for Job, though it is acceptable to his counselors.

"Why do you show partiality toward God?" (13:1-12)

This passage contains one of Job's most profound criticisms of the pastoral care that he has been receiving. He begins very much as he began Chap. 12, protesting that he is not inferior to his counselors, that he knows as much as they do, that they should not talk down to him (vv. 1-2). He wants to make his case with God Almighty, presuming that he will have a better chance in that court than with his friends, who have already concluded that he is guilty of some crime (v. 3). He calls them worthless physicians who cover over the inability to deal with the hard questions by telling lies (v. 4). It would be better if they would be silent (as they were for that first week). Whatever reputation for wisdom they might have had was shattered when they decided to open up their mouths to speak (v. 5).

Job asks them why they lie for God, why they show partiality toward God, why they always take God's side in any theological discussion. Why is Job's suffering the fault of Job and not the responsibility of God? Why do we always blame the human beings when things go wrong and even deny the message of our senses in order to protect God's reputation? Why do Job's counselors feel they must rush in to defend God from the outlandish cries of a despairing human being? Who needs more comfort in a situation like that— God or the poor human being? Job would contend that God can take care of himself. Job needs an intercessor to stand up for him before God. His friends should be less concerned with defending God and more interested in comforting Job. Instead of comfort, he feels condemnation. Even the truth becomes distorted, e.g., they must try to make Job out to look like a heinous sinner—in order that God might be protected.

Job has pointed out a common characteristic of the professional religious counselor. When a sufferer cries out in anguish toward God, we too often rush in to head off the criticism, trying to put God in a good light, unwilling to let the lament run its course. Job contends that God will rebuke us if we show partiality on his behalf (v. 10). Maybe there are times when it would be more appropriate to join in the protest against God's lack of response to

human pain than to try to seek an intellectual solution that always begins with
the assumption that it must be the fault of the human beings.

"I want to make my case directly with God" (13:13-28)

Job is about to give up on his comforters. From now on, they scarcely
hear each other as they talk past each other. Job has decided to throw caution
to the winds and tell God exactly what he has in mind, whatever the outcome
might be (vv. 13-14). Even if God kills him, there is no other hope (v. 15).[19]
Job says he has prepared his case and has confidence that he will be vindicated
(v. 18). Yet he approaches God with great fear (v. 21). He wants a definite
word from God, whether God speaks first or Job speaks first (v. 22). If God
will only let him know what is his transgression (v. 23)! Perhaps there has
been something to what Job's accusers have been saying. At this point, Job
wavers in his claims of innocence. Maybe there is a defect within him that
he has been unable to locate. It could be some sin of his youth (v. 26). If
you go back that far, perhaps there is some sin that God has not forgotten,
even though Job has.

Job has been contending all along that he is not deserving of his suffering.
His friends say that God is not unjust; therefore Job must be suffering for a
reason. If his friends are right, Job wants to know, from God himself, where
the fault lies. Though such a confrontation with God frightens him, he can
see no other way. Surely, the counselors have already shown how useless
they are in providing help.

"Life is short, and not sweet" (14:1-6)

Job repeats thoughts that he has already expressed. Human life is fleeting.
Humans can never be pure before God (vv. 3-4). God knows how long each
person will live and nothing we do can change that (v. 5). It would be best,
then, if God would look away from humans, leave them alone, let them have
their brief time in the sun, and not continue to lay great expectations upon
them (v. 6).

"If only there were life after this one" (14:7-17)

In a beautiful passage, Job contrasts the hope for the emergence of new
life from a felled tree with the lack of hope for a dead human being. "So
man lies down and rises not again; till the heavens are no more he will not
awake, or be roused out of his sleep" (v. 12). A tree will sprout again, but
a man is gone forever. Death is the end, like a permanent sleep. Even that
view of death had some appeal to Job (when he found this life so unpleasant
that even nothingness would be a relief, Chap. 3). But in 14:13-17, Job

indulges in some wishful longing for a life after this one. He hopes against hope that there will be more after this life, that God will redeem him from Sheol after his anger has subsided (v. 13), and that any transgressions God is holding against him will be covered (v. 17) and a new life with God will be possible.

"You destroy a person's hope" (14:18-22)

But it is too good to be true. Job had stood on the threshold of hope. For a moment he toyed with the idea that there is more to existence than this life, the possibility that even a miserable life ending in an early death might have a brighter future. But then the dark mood comes back. Before hope has a chance to grow, it is crushed. As mountains crumble, as water wears away at stones and soil, so God destroys human hope (vv. 18-19). The glimmer of light is gone. Job is back in the pits. The relentless pain of his situation and the belief that God is responsible for it are too much to bear. He has been worn down by the torrential rain of misfortune.

SUMMARY OF SIGNIFICANT THEOLOGICAL AND PASTORAL INSIGHTS

Before we leave our examination of the first cycle of speeches, let us draw together some issues that have special importance for our understanding of suffering and our ministry to the sufferer. We have made brief mention of most of these points as we looked at individual passages. Lest we lose sight of the bigger picture, let us pause here for a few generalities.

1. The mood swings of sufferers

Scholars have often noted the great change between the Job of Chaps. 1–2 and the Job of Chap. 3: the submissive, faithful, stoic Job as over against the despairing and questioning Job. Could this be the same person? Could a sufferer change that much? Many have assumed that such sharply divergent pictures of Job must come from different authors. Is it not possible that the same person had a change of mood? A sufferer may appear to be taking it well, the patient who has just learned of a terminal cancer may still be smiling and talking about the goodness of God. But in the next day or the next week or the next year, the walls come crashing down and one is left in a pile of rubble with no defense left. And then the relatives and friends wonder what has happened to cause such a change.

There is no universal pattern of response to calamity. There are no stages through which everyone will go in neat order. Job submits to God and accepts

his fate. But later he cannot stand it any more. He alternates between submission and fighting against God for putting him in this situation. He is caught
between fear of God and trust in God. He remembers how it used to be and
speaks in tender phrases about God's power and love and protection. Then
the reality of his present suffering dawns on him again and he strikes out at
God in anger. Even though people reach the point of submission to God and
acceptance of their fate, there is no guarantee that they will stay on that calm
plateau and not fall off again into despair.

We do not know what will happen to us in times of great distress. We
hope that we will remain rational, that faith will not desert us, that we will
be a good example to family and friends. In the first numbing time after the
disaster strikes, we may well be able to keep up a good front and impress
those around us. But in the cold of the night and the agony of loneliness,
ugly and hostile and terrifying thoughts seek to take control of our minds.
Some days we can beat them back, but on other days they take over. The
process may go on a long time. A widow may finally think she has "gotten
over" the death of her husband of 40 years and then something reminds her
of her loss, and the dark cloud closes in on her again.

The Job of Chap. 2 could be the same man as the Job of Chap. 3. The
Job who denounces God for his lack of justice in Chap. 9 can speak tenderly
of God's providence in Chap. 10. The Job who stands on the brink of hope
in the middle of Chap. 14 sees it all washing away by the end of Chap. 14.
If only we could hold on to those glorious times of assurance and hold back
the recurrence of doubt and anxiety! But, like Job, our mood swings are often
beyond our control.

2. Job's understanding of death

There will be more to say on this subject later in the book of Job. But
up to the end of the first cycle, we can say this much:

(a) Job does not expect anything beyond this life. He sounds like most
of the Old Testament writers in his skepticism about any meaningful existence
following death. He speaks of death as a place of sleep, a place from which
no one returns, a place that is dark and gloomy (e.g., Chap. 3; 7:7-10; 10:21-
22; and 14:12).

(b) Even this picture of death could be a word of comfort if things are
bad enough. In his lowest times, Job even thinks of death as a relief, a way
out of present misery (3:11-19). We worry when a depressed person begins
to speak of the attractiveness of death as compared to life. And yet, when a
very old or very sick person speaks of death as a rest and release from bodily
pain, we can appreciate that and treat it as a word of hope.

(c) By Chap. 14 Job begins to show a deep longing for something more than the finality of death. It is clear to him that God's justice is not always going to work out in this life. If a good person has a life filled with misery and dies without ever seeing better days, then there is no way that that person can receive justice. If this life is all that there is, then innocent suffering is a terrible thing. There is no time to rectify the wrong done to someone like Job. Job had spoken several times about the shortness of life (e.g., 7:6; 9:25-26; 14:1-2). In Chap. 14 he almost lets himself believe that a dead human being can live again. Such a possibility would provide time for his good name to be regained, for his relationship with God to be renewed, and for God's justice (with regard to both the innocent and the wicked) to be executed.

Later biblical writers will be more confident in proclaiming belief in life after death. To Job, it is still illusory hope, too good to be true, a belief beyond his grasp.

3. "Good answers" that are "bad answers"

What is a good thing to say to someone like Job who has just experienced personal disaster? That was the question faced by Job's friends. And so they sought the most helpful words they knew. They consulted the past, the religious traditions of their spiritual ancestors, the best words of wisdom from the sages of old. How had other people who went before them dealt with these same questions that Job is raising? The explanations that they came up with were not that bad. We have not been able to improve on them very much over the years. Eliphaz, in particular, is a wise man who spells out, often in lovely language, the best-known explanations for the presence of human suffering: "Suffering is the result of human sin. There are cause-and-effect relationships in the way the world is constituted so that we cannot act in a way which runs counter to those rules without having to pay the consequence. God is continually at work in the world to see that this system works and people are properly rewarded and punished. All of us are sinners so that even the suffering of seemingly innocent people is not a contradiction to the effectiveness of God's justice. Further, it may be useful to think of suffering as educative, teaching us something about ourselves that we might not have learned without the severity of such a test." These are "good answers" from Eliphaz.

Even those less able counselors, Bildad and Zophar, spoke the truth· at times. "God does have power. There are limits to human understanding of God" (e.g., 11:7-12). "We ought to gain from the teachings of our ancestors and not be so brash as to think that our own experiences are somehow normative for understanding the universe" (8:7-10).

Sometimes Job even says the same things that his counselors say, e.g., about God's power and the inability of humans to understand God fully or bring God into account. Moreover, as we noted earlier, when God himself finally speaks God will also make similar points about the gap between human understanding and the divine mysteries.

In short, the counselors are not all bad. Their words of comfort and encouragement are not, in and of themselves, wrong. They speak much truth. Many people have found comfort in the words spoken by Eliphaz (less so with Bildad and Zophar). And yet Job heard only condemnation and evidence of a lack of understanding of his plight. An answer that may be helpful to one person may not be to another. An answer that is helpful to a person today may not be helpful tomorrow. Not all suffering has the same cause. Some of my suffering may indeed be the result of my own folly, stupidity, bad health habits, inability to handle stress, or (if you will) sin. But I may encounter other suffering in my life which does not fit into that category, and I will be insulted, offended, and condemned by you if you insist on interpreting my suffering on the basis of a rigid doctrine which might work elsewhere but does not fit my context.

There is great danger in pronouncing a meaning on someone else's suffering. Even a profound insight that has helped us greatly in our own personal struggles with the pains of life may sound like a pious platitude—or worse—to someone else. "Good answers" are not always good. Other factors will determine whether this was the right time or place for such a word, such as the sufferer's own faith history, relevance to the reality of this *specific* example of suffering, and the relationship that exists between the sufferer and the counselor.

4. The futility of arguing theological doctrines with a sufferer

Job and his three friends had great difficulty because they were approaching the subject of suffering from two different levels. Job was the actual sufferer. When he talked about suffering he was talking about *himself* in relationship to God. He was very much on the "feeling" level, even as he raised his "Why?" questions. His counselors, on the other hand, were dealing with suffering primarily as an intellectual problem that needed to be solved, a complex set of difficult questions which required a rational answer. When Job cried out "Why me?" he was lamenting his loss of health and property, his feeling of alienation and loneliness, and he was hoping someone would hear him and respond warmly to his cry of pain. Instead, his counselors heard his "Why me?" as a theoretical question which they should try to answer. When Job made disparaging remarks about God's justice, he was hoping for compassion. Instead he got arguments, along with condemnation for getting himself into trouble and for daring to question it once it had come.

Particularly in Chap. 6 (see vv. 3 and 26) Job admits his words are rash. He knows he is speaking irrationally, out of great pain. He does not want to be forever accountable for what he has been saying out of great distress. He wants comfort, not explanations of suffering which protect God and condemn Job. When his friends respond, he finds himself being drawn deeper into arguments about the validity of the doctrine of retribution and the reliability of God's justice.

There is a time for intellectual discussion about the meaning of suffering. There are profound questions here which should concern any thinking person. But the time for such a discussion is probably not during the trauma of great suffering. In the immediacy of suffering, almost any effort to make sense out of what is happening seems trivial and unhelpful. If it takes the direction of defending the image of God at the expense of human beings, it may even become harmful. Though sufferers may bombard the would-be comforter with "Why?" questions, it may be best to side-step the intellectual level for a time and deal with the sufferer at the emotional level. Among other things, this would mean acceptance of the sufferer, without trying to correct or condemn thoughts which may seem unorthodox or illogical. It would also mean the courage to resist trying to say more than we know (not an easy restraint for many religious types) and pretending that there are easy answers to such hard questions. And it would mean to stop treating the sufferer as if he or she were a problem to be solved rather than a human being to be loved and comforted.

5. The ambiguity of God's constant presence

Is it good for us human beings that God takes such an interest in us? Is it to our advantage that God is always there, knowing all that we do, even what we think? Is it comforting to know that God is very concerned about how human beings behave and will distribute rewards and punishments in order to prod us into obedience to his will? God's omnipresence is at least a *mixed* blessing in the mind of Job. Several times he asks God to let him alone, to quit bothering him, to let him die in peace (e.g., 7:16; 10:20; and 14:6). Psalm 8 (see also Ps. 144:3) sings the praise of a God who thinks that human beings are so important that God pays special attention to them and assigns them dominion over the whole creation. Job, in 7:17-19, distorts Ps. 8:4 into a piece of bad news. God is too preoccupied with humans, always finding ways to test them, never giving them any privacy under his watchful eye. Job asks what harm it does to God if a human sins. What can poor mortals do to God so that God treats them as potentially dangerous enemies that must be kept under constant guard (7:20; see also 7:12)?

The certainty that God knows everything you are doing can be either good news or bad news. If you need the reassurance of God's presence in your life to bring blessings and to watch and protect you from harm and to guide you into a good life, then it is good news. If you have committed some sin which you do not want God to discover or if you feel burdened by demands for perfection or if you think of God primarily as a celestial judge dispensing rewards and punishments to good and bad little children—then, as for Job, the belief in the constant presence of God can become oppressive and extremely discomforting.

6. The lament "carried too far"

In 6:4 Job says, "For the arrows of the Almighty are in me; my spirit drinks their poison; the terrors of God are arrayed against me." In 9:20-24 Job accuses God of being unjust, indifferent to the plight of the innocent, and turning the world over to the power of the wicked. Should a person talk to God like that? God doesn't poison people. God does not favor wicked people over good people. Like Job's counselors, many of us have the compulsion to correct that kind of thinking, not to let such words lie there without being answered (see 4:2; 8:2-3; and 11:2-3). Though the writer of the book of Job certainly is on Job's side rather than the side of the counselors, many readers of the book find themselves drifting over to the point of view of the counselors. They, too, begin to wonder about Job's response to his suffering. Is it not excessive? If he can talk to God like that, maybe there really is something the matter with him after all. He seems so preoccupied with himself. He is a moaner, a complainer. He is hostile toward other people. Certainly he is not very kind to his friends who have made such a special effort to come to console him. To be sure, people need time to grieve, to come to grips with the reality of their pain, but shouldn't they get over that quickly and turn their lives over to God and cut out all this negative thinking?

Our religious tradition as Christians has often urged us to stifle lament. We have been told to praise and thank God no matter what is happening to us. The strong, silent, stoic, submissive, noncomplaining person has been the model of piety which we are to emulate. The Job of the first two chapters has managed to obscure our vision of the Job of the rest of the book.

Does Job go too far? It seemed so to his counselors as they responded to his words. It seems so to most Christians who read past Chap. 2 and interpret it from their perspective on the impropriety of lament. But Job's words are not that unusual for the Old Testament. Other figures, particularly Jeremiah, moan and groan and challenge God for the suffering God has inflicted on them. These are common themes in the lament psalms where God's justice is challenged, the wicked are condemned in very hostile terms, and human complaints are recited over and over in vivid and gruesome detail.

The point is that the Old Testament does allow lament. If a human being's relationship with God means anything, if we are to have the freedom to be honest with God, then there must be room for lament. We are not always flying high, full of a sense of God's grace and care, with no doubts about God and what God is doing. There are times when it would be very strange indeed not to speak in lament, for example the death of a child, the loss of all the crops in a hailstorm, being fired from a job at age 55, or learning that one has less than three months to live. The lament allows one to talk honestly to God even at times like these and not only when we can be grateful for our many blessings.

But how far is "too far"? Who is going to decide that? The local clergyman? Eliphaz or Bildad or Zophar? Who are we to step in another's shoes and say, "OK. This has gone far enough. You must shape up now and quit babying yourself and start being grateful for what you still have." How far is "too far"? When does lament become blasphemy or renunciation or cursing of God? In a way, the question is irrelevant. If a person still needs to lament, then it has not gone too far. It must continue. In the meantime, if the words verge on blasphemy or denial of God's goodness, we should remember that they probably bother us more than they bother God. A God who is willing to bear our sins on the cross can surely tolerate abusive language from a tormented sufferer who, under great pressure, utters words which would never be said in more pleasant circumstances. God may be pained by our inability to trust God. But God will never abandon us for our intemperate outbursts. God would rather have us continue to talk with God, even though the words be strained and accusatory, than have us draw away in disgust and disbelief. The lament keeps the conversation open, and as long as that happens there is hope that we will be able to hear when God speaks.

4

The Second and Third Cycles of Speeches (Job 15-27)

A. THE SECOND CYCLE (JOB 15-21)

Eliphaz (Chapter 15)

All three of Job's friends have had their say. And Job has responded to each of them. But the talk is far from over. Each of the three now comes back for a second try at Job. Eliphaz again is first. He had made a thoughtful, gentle, though somewhat condescending and mildly condemning presentation the first time. Now, after listening to the way Job has been talking, he has probably changed his mind about Job. In the first speech, Eliphaz seemed troubled by the apparent goodness of Job and he struggled to reconcile this with his view of suffering as retribution for sin. By the time the first cycle ended, Eliphaz had seen a display of Job's nastiness, hostility, nearly blasphemous statements about God, and sharp criticism of his three friends. Job has given himself away by his own words and there is no need to be so gentle with him any more.

"Your own words give you away" (15:1-6)

Eliphaz begins by accusing Job of arguing in windy, empty, unprofitable words. We should remind ourselves that Job himself (6:26) admitted that his words were wind but he asked that he not be reproved on the basis of words spoken during his time of torment. But Eliphaz and the others have not heeded that caution. They are arguing with Job over the content and are not responding to his need for a friendly hearing.

In v. 4, Eliphaz says that Job is "doing away with the fear of God and hindering meditation before God." Job's outbursts, questioning of God's justice, and unwillingness to accept traditional religious consolation is setting a bad example. If everyone were like Job, if all sufferers followed his example, if people turned against God every time a little trouble came their way, then there would be no proper piety. Further, if God really is unjust, as Job has been saying, then the simple faithful folk would lose their motivation for being obedient to God's commands and ordinances. If Job had his way, nobody would fear and love and serve God any more.

In vv. 5 and 6, Eliphaz suggests that Job "protests too much" about his innocence. Like an amateur psychologist who has had the introductory course in psychology or one quarter of clinical pastoral education, Eliphaz presumes to read a guilty conscience into the "overreaction" and intensity of Job's rejection of any personal responsibility for his present suffering. "He must really be guilty or he wouldn't be making such a big fuss about defending himself." Job has given the whole thing away by what he has been saying. There is no need to condemn him. He has done it to himself by his words. Though he claims to be innocent, his true self is gradually emerging in the way he has lashed out at God and other human beings in his time of suffering. To be sure, he seemed to be a good man, but now we begin to see what Job is really like.

"Quit being so high and mighty, Job" (15:7-13)

In this section, Eliphaz becomes quite defensive. He and his two fellow counselors have been personally attacked by Job. It is not easy to remain cool and serene and nonthreatened when your integrity has been questioned. "To be sure, Job has suffered a lot and he doesn't mean all that he says and maybe he's really angry with God or the world and he's taking it out on me and I ought not to take it so seriously." But, in the heat of the moment, it is hard to hold back and be that magnanimous. Suppose that Eliphaz was a professional religious counselor. Suppose he takes great pride in his wisdom, his knowledge of the tradition, his ability to bring consoling words to those in trouble. He has always been well received. Grateful recipients of his comfort have told him how much they appreciated the help that he brought in their time of need. And now Job implies that he is a worthless physician who abandons those in trouble and doesn't know anything but the warmed-over platitudes that everyone else knows already (see especially Chap. 13). Why shouldn't Eliphaz feel under attack and fight back against such accusations?

Who does Job think he is anyway? Was he the first man to be born in the world, standing around and watching God create the world, picking up valuable wisdom that no one else could possibly know (v. 7)? Has he listened to God's council (like a prophet who overhears what is going on in heaven) or is he the personification of wisdom itself (v. 8)? Job had asked the counselors what they know that he doesn't (12:1-3 and 13:1-2), and now Eliphaz turns the question back on Job. What does he know that they don't know (v. 9)? They have been around a while, too, and some of them (maybe all of them) are even older than Job's father (v. 10). So that makes Job a mere youngster who has not had nearly as many years of living as those counseling him and yet presumes that he can defy the wisdom of the ages on the basis of his limited experience.

Eliphaz asks Job if the consolations of God are "too small" for him (v. 11). "We have been speaking words of comfort to you, even being gentle and patient. Why then do you not accept those words? What is making you so angry?" (vv. 12-13). Eliphaz has very closely identified himself with his message. He feels threatened. A rejection of his "comforting" word is perceived as a rejection of Eliphaz himself. Further, Eliphaz has assumed that the words that he is bringing are actually God's words. Therefore, to refuse those words is not only to reject the messenger (Eliphaz) but it is a repudiation of God himself. Job has been put down one more time. He *is* angry. Eliphaz is right about that. He wishes he could accept a consoling word and stop feeling this way and thinking such outrageous thoughts. But wishing it will not make it so. And more of the doctrine of retribution, peddled by Eliphaz and the others, packaged as if it were a special delivery letter directly from God, will not help remove the anger that Job feels—both toward the counselors and (no thanks to them) toward God.

"Humans can never be clean nor trustworthy" (15:14-16)

Eliphaz returns to a point he had made earlier (4:17-19). All human beings are sinners. Humans can never be righteous. Even angels do not meet God's standards for cleanliness, so what chance is there that mortal men and women can possibly live up to God's criteria for perfection? This "worm theology" (all human beings are terrible and worthless and corrupt) does provide a way for Eliphaz to continue to believe in suffering as the result of sin since all people (even one like Job who, on the surface, looks as though he might be innocent) are sinners, after all. This statement of God's lack of trust in humanity seems a far cry from what God was saying to Satan in Chaps. 1 and 2. God had singled out Job as one who would not waver from loyalty to God even in time of great suffering. God, in fact, had designated Job as one who could be trusted. Now Eliphaz tells Job that God trusts no creature, least of all humans, and (perhaps implicit in this) certainly not someone like Job.

Later, Bildad will raise the same point as Eliphaz, even using the words "maggot" and "worm" to describe what human beings are like (25:6).

"There is no hope for the wicked" (15:17-35)

Now Eliphaz enters into a discourse about the inevitable fate of wicked people. As in previous conversation, Eliphaz claims to be speaking both from personal observation (v. 17) and his study of what the wise teachers of the past have handed down to us (v. 18). Wicked people will not be able to get away with it (vv. 30-32). God's justice is under attack if the innocent people suffer (as Job claims) but there is also an injustice if wicked people are not punished. There is no justice if one can go through life without paying any attention to God's commands—stealing, lying, cheating, taking advantage of the powerless—and still go to the grave in an affluent old age with never a feeling of remorse or even a small hint of God's vengeance on such behavior. The prosperity of the wicked is as big a challenge to God's fairness as is the suffering of the innocent. Often sufferers complain that they do not deserve such severe treatment. In the effort to push that point, lamenters (as Job) often exaggerate their innocence and point to other people who are worse, bigger sinners, more wicked, more deserving of punishment—if God is looking for people to punish. Job has certainly been maintaining his innocence but, so far, he has not been saying much about the fate of the wicked. Eliphaz initiates this subject and the rest of the counselors and Job then pick up the theme; it dominates the discussion through the rest of the second cycle and into the third.

Is Eliphaz talking in general about wicked people in an abstract argument about God's justice? Or is he thinking of Job when he describes the wicked man whom God will finally bring to account? When Eliphaz condemns one who "has stretched forth his hand against God, and bids defiance to the Almighty" (v. 25), is he talking in general terms or is he thinking of Job himself? "If the shoe fits, wear it." Certainly Job would be likely to hear this as another condemnation by Eliphaz, another reproach because he had dared to challenge God.

Job's Response (Chapters 16–17)

"You are miserable comforters" (16:1-6)

Job has another chance to tell his comforters how bad they are. They say nothing new (v. 2) and they love to argue in windy words (v. 3). Job then goes on to point out the difference in his situation as compared to theirs. If he could change places with them, he could appear to be as wise as they. He could still have the confidence that he had something profound to say and still live with the illusion that his words were actually comforting (vv. 4-5). But it is different when you are the one whose world has fallen apart. No arguments help. Some are worse than others, but none of them helps. The pain is a constant, no matter what rational explanation is given for it. For the counselors, Job presents a problem that they would like to solve; they search for words to give it some meaning so they can leave and go home. But Job is stuck in the pain—no explanation will remove it. If Job decides to speak and argue against his friends, the pain is still there. If he refrains and bites his lip and holds back the anger and frustration and fears, the pain is still there (v. 6). There is no getting away from it. Sooner or later the others can go away from him and that's the end of it. But for Job, there is no end of it.

Explanations of pain and other suffering that work very well in the classroom, from the pulpit, as part of our system of making sense out of the world, tend to dissipate into triviality when suffering hits us in our own personal lives. What had seemed a creative profundity is transformed into a vacuous platitude. For a counselor to keep pushing a pious generalization as if it were still a profound insight is absolutely no help at all. Job's perspective, as a sufferer, is much different from that of his friends, and they are not understanding each other at all.

"Both God and humans are out to get me" (16:7-17)

This is one of the most painful outbursts from Job in the whole book. God is the enemy, the adversary of Job. "Even though other humans have participated in my suffering by judging my situation as just punishment (v. 8) or by mocking, insulting, and striking me (v. 10), God is really the enemy. It is God who has worn me out (v. 7), torn me in his hatred (v. 9), and turned me over to the hands of wicked people (v. 11)." In vv. 12-14, Job uses vivid imagery of breaking, seizing, slashing, attacking, and more, to describe the violence which Job feels on the part of God. It is terrible to think about God in such a way. Even when human beings are clearly the cause of his suffering, Job blames God because God gave them permission to do what they are doing (v. 11). Where does one turn for help if God is a hostile enemy?

It is interesting that Job closes this awful lament with the affirmation that his prayer is pure (v. 17). Is it possible to say such harsh words about God and still claim that your prayer is pure? Job thought so. With our discomfort with even relatively mild forms of lament, we would probably join in the chorus led by Eliphaz and suggest that Job's own words condemn him (15:6). Job is terribly confused and hurt and his picture of God is obviously out of kilter. But his prayer is still "pure," perhaps because it is still an honest and open communication which dares to lay even such awful thoughts and feelings before the Almighty and trust that they will be heard.

"I desperately need vindication" (16:18-22)

In the preceding verses, Job had been talking as if he were being murdered, and the murderer was none other than God. Job cries out that his death should be vindicated, not covered up, put to rest, suppressed (v. 18). As in Gen. 4:10, the blood of one who has been murdered cries out to God asking for vengeance. In the story of Cain and Abel, God hears the cry. But if God himself is the killer, then to whom will the cry be addressed? Who will hear and intercede with God? Who is the witness in heaven (v. 19)? Earlier (9:33) Job had complained that there is no umpire to decide disputes between God and humans. When God is acting unjustly, there is no one to call God to account. We humans are not able to contend against those odds. God, it seems, has all the power.

So, who is the witness in heaven? Is this some strange prophetic witness to a preexistent Jesus? There were times when the church felt free to make such interpretations, but now we are much more cautious. Though we can see connections between Job's need and the role later fulfilled by Jesus, we know that only because we know the story of Jesus, and the writer of the book of Job did not have that information. Most scholars identify the witness with God himself. Job is calling upon God to witness to himself, just as God would listen and make a judgment in a case between two human neighbors (v. 21). Job seems to be asking God himself to stand between God and humans in order to settle their dispute. Job, though he has just uttered a horrendous list of atrocities committed by God against him, still finds that he must appeal to that same God.

Though crushed by God, he still turns to God as his only hope. Though temporarily overwhelmed by the image of God as violent enemy, Job has not entirely lost what he once knew about God. He appeals to that earlier vision of a God who is compassionate and merciful and just, the God he used to know back in the good days before all the trouble started. Maybe that God will hear his pleas and make his case for him with the other God who has been hurting him. Job, of course, still believes in only one God, but he is torn by his different perceptions of God. At the same time, God is both enemy and also the only chance for vindication, redemption, deliverance.

Job expects to die soon (v. 22). Perhaps this comment is meant to inspire God to act before it is too late.

"My good name is gone" (17:1-10)

Job goes on to talk about his loss of reputation, largely because his calamities are seen as payment for some sin. "God would not do this to him if there were not some good reason." God has made Job a "byword of the peoples," "one before whom men spit" (v. 6). The Hebrew word translated "byword" in the RSV is used in other places to indicate the judgment that will come upon the people of Judah when God sends them into exile (e.g., Deut. 28:37; 1 Kings 9:7; 2 Chron. 7:20; and Jer. 24:9). As Judah was to be an example, a parable, a vivid illustration of God's dealing with sinful humans, so Job would be seen as an example of a victim of God's justice. Though the dating of the book of Job is shaky at best, the period of the exile would be a time when such a book would meet a very important need. "If we are God's chosen people, why are we suffering like this? It is not enough to say that we deserve it. There are many worse people in the world than we." Though the story of Job is the story of an individual innocent sufferer, it certainly raises questions which would be vital for an understanding of the corporate suffering of the whole nation.

"I am left without hope" (17:11-16)

The Hebrew in this section is difficult and we cannot be sure exactly what Job is saying. Nevertheless, it is clear that Job is convinced that there is no longer any hope for restoration for him within this life. Though his comforters speak as if there may be "light at the end of the tunnel" (v. 12 may mean something like that) if Job repents and turns his life over to God, Job is convinced that there is nothing ahead of him but death, Sheol, the grave, and the worms that will eat his flesh (vv. 13-14). There is no hope— either for this life or for anything after this life has ended. If the best you can look forward to is a family consisting of the grave as your father and worms as your mother and sister, then you are indeed in a sad state.

The bitterness and loneliness and alienation and depression of Job in Chaps. 16–17 is among the worst in the whole book. Job has virtually hit rock bottom.

Bildad (Chapter 18)

Now Bildad returns for his second chance. In his first speech (Chap. 8), Bildad was most noteworthy for his uncritical acceptance of the doctrine of retribution, his suggestion that Job's children probably deserved what they got, and his admonition to Job not to reject the wisdom passed on by our ancestors simply because the ancient truths don't harmonize nicely with his immediate experience. Bildad does not inspire confidence as an innovative thinker. As long as the world keeps operating the way he expects it to work, Bildad will get along just fine. But when new situations challenge the old ways of thinking, Bildad hangs on fiercely to the tradition regardless of what his senses tell him.

"Why are we stupid in your sight?" (18:1-4)

Job's attacks on the counselors have had their effect. There was a considerable change in Eliphaz from his first speech to his second. Bildad, like Eliphaz, begins his second speech with defensive words. Job had accused his friends of talking down to him (e.g., in Chaps. 12 and 13). In 15:7-10, Eliphaz complained that Job thinks he knows more than they do, even though they represent wisdom accumulated through many years of living. And now Bildad wonders why Job treats them as if they are stupid animals (v. 3). For Bildad and the others, the focus is no longer on Job and his suffering. They are becoming more and more preoccupied with their own words, their own doctrinal positions, even their own reputation as wise and able counselors. There is no longer much chance that Job will be helped, because everyone has become more interested in protecting his own position than in hearing what the other has to say.

Bildad accuses Job of tearing himself (v. 4). Though Job described in great length how God had attacked and wounded him (16:12-14), Bildad raises the possibility that the wounds are self-inflicted. It is not only (in line with Bildad's view of retribution) that Job has brought on his own suffering. Job has actually made the suffering much more severe than need be because he has refused to accept responsibility, face the truth openly, and come to God asking for forgiveness. Hanging on to his exaggerated claims for innocence, Job has made God into a violent enemy rather than a friend. Further, Job acts as if the whole world should change for his benefit (v. 4b, c). Should laws of cause and effect which have operated in the universe since the creation be suddenly set aside simply because Job can't understand them anymore? Who does Job think he is anyway?

There is, of course, some truth to what Bildad says. Job is angry and hurt and is getting himself into a deep hole in his relationship with God. God looks cruel instead of loving and Job does not know where to turn. But, even if Bildad is not entirely incorrect in his analysis, what has he done to help Job out of this dilemma? One more reproach surely will not improve the situation.

"The terrible fate of the wicked" (18:5-21)

As we have already said, a dominant theme through the second and third cycles is the question of whether or not wicked people are properly punished. (Eliphaz raised this issue in 15:17-35.) The three counselors, seeking to be consistent in their belief in the doctrine of retribution, argue that sooner or later God will repay the evildoer. Job will be forced to argue the negative side of this proposition (with great eloquence, as we will see in Chap. 21).

As we asked earlier regarding Eliphaz (in Chap. 15), one wonders whether Bildad is arguing theoretically about the ultimate destruction of the wicked and the justification of the doctrine of retribution, naively oblivious to the negative effect this would have on poor Job. Or is Bildad deliberately and cruelly making reference to Job in an explicit way? Job would certainly understand it as an attack on him when Bildad's list of the calamities of the ungodly person sounds very much like what has happened to him. "By disease his skin is consumed" (v. 13a) and "He has no offspring or descendant among his people, and no survivor where he used to live" (v. 19).

It is possible that this passage contains some allusions to the fate of the people of Israel in exile. Particularly vv. 14 to 21 could be understood as a picture of what it is like to be sent into exile, away from roots, tradition, family. At least the exilic experience could have given the poet some of the images which he uses.

Bildad almost seems to enjoy listing the disasters which will befall the impious ones. We can perhaps see a touch of hostility toward those who thought they were escaping God's attention but will finally be made to squirm when God catches up with them. Good religious folks, like Bildad, are sometimes at their most imaginative and creative peak as they articulate the terrible punishment that God has in store for "all those sinners out there." We will return to this seeming incongruity—good religious folk taking delight in the suffering of other human beings.

Job's Response (Chapter 19)

"How long will you torment me?" (19:1-6)

Job again is critical of his "comforters," though this time with less sharp-

ness and sarcasm than in earlier speeches (e.g., in Chaps. 12 and 13). Bildad
had begun both his speeches (Chaps. 8 and 18) with the expression "How
long?" How long will Job continue to speak in windy and impious words?
Now Job turns the same expression back on the counselors and wonders "how
long" they will continue to torment him with their dismal attempts at bringing
comfort (v. 2). They have reproached him ten times (v. 3). The number *ten*
is probably symbolic for "often," or "repeated," or some such meaning. So
far, Job has listened to five speeches, not ten, though if someone wanted to
find ten insults within those speeches, it would be an easy task. In fact, it
would be difficult to limit the number to ten.

Job has felt condemnation, condescension, and reproof from his friends
from the opening speech of Eliphaz. Sometimes words that appear to be helpful
and spoken out of concern for the sufferer actually are perceived as insults.
And the sad part is that the counselors do not even know what effect all this
has had on Job. They are not even ashamed of the way they have treated him
(v. 3). Rather, they are convinced that the problem lies with Job, in his refusal
to receive with a humble spirit their well intentioned words of consolation
and advice.

What if Job has actually erred (v. 4)? What if he has in fact committed
some sin which is serious enough to bring on all these troubles in his life?
What if his thinking is mixed up and his theology needs some straightening
out? Even if all that is true (and Job probably is not admitting that it is true
but is only talking hypothetically), what difference does that make to Job's
friends? How can that be any danger to them? Why should they be threatened
by Job's errors so that they reply with such vehemence to any critique of their
own position or what they perceive as an attack on God? Job is telling them
that this is between God and him (v. 6).

Job has almost reached the final stage in his dismissal of the counselors.
There is no point any longer to share his pain and anger with them. They do
not understand. They always take God's side. They take Job's humiliation
and his reaction to it as proof of the rightness of their own doctrine of retribution (v. 5). The speeches between Job and the others will continue for a
time, but more and more they will be talking past each other instead of to
each other.

"God has done it to me" (19:7-12)

Job is convinced that all that has happened to him is God's doing. In
Job's mind, it is part of the definition of God that God can indeed do whatever
God wants and nothing happens unless God wills it. Therefore, God is directly
accountable for Job's suffering. In these verses (similar to what Job says in

16:7-17), Job recites a litany of offenses which God has committed against him. "I am not answered when I protest injustice" (v. 7). "God has confined me so that there is no way to move, no place to go" (v. 8). "He has taken away my glory, my respect" (v. 9). "He breaks me down and he uproots my hope" (v. 10). "He has fired up his wrath and counts me as an adversary" (v. 11). "He even calls out his army to besiege me" (v. 12). (Again we find language reminiscent of the experience of exile: being besieged, destroyed, and uprooted to another land.)

Job's friends do not understand him and God is the cause of all his trouble. To whom, then, is Job to turn? Chapters 16 and 19 are perhaps the most bitter of all Job's laments. The sense of alienation from God is at its worst. In both of these chapters, Job is so outraged, terrified, and angry with God that he can scarcely pray. He talks in the third person, about what God has done to him, as if he were telling someone else (though his friends don't want to hear), rather than to tell God himself. His thoughts about God are so awful that all he can do is mutter about it rather than take it directly to God in prayer.

"All humans have rejected me" (19:13-20)

Even when Job's friends and family turn against him, Job interprets this as God's doing. "He has put my brethren far from me" (v. 13a). Perhaps they had some choice in the matter, but his repulsiveness (which drives them away from him) is God's responsibility.

This is a touching statement of Job's loneliness and alienation from all human comfort at precisely the time when that is most needed. He lists in order all those who used to be close to him but who now have left him, failed him, forgotten him, ignored him, been repulsed by him, despised him, and abhorred him. The persons named include his kinfolk and close friends (v. 14), guests and servants in his house (vv. 15-16), his wife and brothers (v. 17), young children (v. 18), and all his intimate friends whom he loved (v. 19). It is sadly true that many sufferers feel like Job when trouble hits them. Old friends and family do not know how to react to a person who has been touched by tragedy, by illness, by despair. They may even be repulsed by bodily changes, deterioration in appearance, unpleasant body odors. They may be worried because they will give themselves away by their facial expressions or by a verbal reaction that they cannot hold back. Perhaps they avoid the sufferer because they do not know what to say when the inevitable questions about why this is happening are raised. Maybe they have tried to stay close to the sufferer, but the endless despair, complaining, bitterness, and hostility is simply wearing them out. Suffering people, like Job, are not easy to get along with. If there are not enough reasons why even loved ones avoid them, they will provide more reasons by their unpleasantness. It becomes a self-fulfilling prophecy: the more Job complains about loved ones who let him down, the more likely they are to do just that.

Verse 20b has provided our language with a familiar proverbial phrase: "And I have escaped by the skin of my teeth." The precise meaning of this image in the Hebrew is impossible to recover. Some have taken it to mean that Job's bones stuck out through his skin like teeth.[20] Most likely Job is saying that he has suffered so much that he has just barely survived. After all he has been through, it is a wonder that he is alive at all.

"Don't be like God. Have pity" (19:21-22)

Job had begun this speech with a plea for his friends to stop tormenting him. Now he returns to that theme again. One more time he asks for them to have pity on him. God has been hurting him, Job feels (v. 21b), and he urges his friends not to be like God, not to chase after him with an unrelenting need to chastise that is never completely satisfied. Let God do the punishing. That is enough for Job to worry about without the friends joining in the act.

These words from Job are disturbing. Usually we are told to be more like God and less like humans, more loving and giving and less self-centered. But Job tells his comforters to be *less* like God. These words give us another glimpse into the distorted image of God which has come to predominate in the mind of Job. God is unjust, indifferent to the cry of the offended party, an adversary who pursues specific human beings as if he has a personal vendetta against them.

"I know that my Redeemer lives" (19:23-27)

This section contains some of the most familiar words of the entire book of Job. Unfortunately, the precise meaning of this passage is not clear. There are problems with the Hebrew text and there are other ambiguities that remain even when we can be reasonably certain about the Hebrew word in question. The difficulties are particularly acute with v. 26.

Job hopes that he will not be forgotten, that his words spoken in defense of his own integrity will not disappear when he dies. He wishes that his words could be written in a book (which, of course, they were—the book of Job which we are reading) or inscribed on a rock so that they could be seen by future generations. Thus, Job hopes that people will come to know the truth about him, that they will hear his side of the story in his dispute with God, that they will remember him as a good man who was treated unfairly rather than as a bad man who was rightfully suffering for his sins (vv. 23-24).

The "Redeemer" (v. 25) in Hebrew tradition is the next of kin who performs certain acts on behalf of a relative who is not able to take care of them himself, usually because of death. For example the redeemer (gō' ēl) may be the one who avenges the blood of a family member who has been murdered (as Num. 35:19-21; see Job 16:18-19), or who buys back property that might otherwise be lost to the family because of debt (e.g., Lev. 25:25), or who marries a widow in order to provide the deceased man with descendants (e.g., Boaz in the book of Ruth; see also Mark 12:18-27). Sometimes there seems to be no hope for a human being who will step forward to take the part of the next of kin in these situations, and God himself is implored to become the "Redeemer," the "Avenger," the "Vindicator." This same Hebrew word is used to describe God in Pss. 19:14 and 78:35, in Jer. 50:34, and several times in Isaiah (including 41:14; 43:14; 44:6, 24; 47:4; and 48:17).

When Job asserts his hope that a Redeemer will finally vindicate his good name, he is probably thinking of God. There have been no human volunteers for such a task. God appears to be the only hope, even though Job continues to talk as if God is the one who has caused all his trouble (especially in Chap. 16 and here in 19). For Job God is both the enemy against whom he needs to be avenged and also the one who must do the avenging.

The difficulties in interpreting this passage increase when we get to vv. 26 and 27. One can find great differences of opinion among those who have written commentaries on these verses. A couple of things seem relatively certain out of all this confusion. Job hopes to be vindicated by God himself *and* he expects to know about it. Job expects to see God, who is now on his side and speaking on his behalf (vv. 26b-27). The most debated question here is whether or not this vindication on the part of God will come before Job has died or after he has died. The Hebrew in v. 26a is of little help since it could read either "in my flesh" or "without my flesh." Does Job hope for a vindication before he dies or is there no chance that it will come until after his death? If it comes while he is yet alive, then obviously his desire to see it will be possible. But if it does not come till a later time, after he is dead and gone and sleeping away in Sheol, then how will he know about it? Does Job hope for a resurrection in which he comes back to life so that he can enjoy the renewal of his good name? Or, perhaps, would it be only a brief arousal from the slumber of Sheol so that he could savor the moment of victory and then drop off to perpetual rest again? There is no certainty what Job has in mind here. He occasionally arrives at the brink of a belief in life after death (as in Chap. 14), but more often speaks as if this life is all that there is. Though he is not explicit about it in Chap. 19, Job comes very close to allowing himself the comfort of belief in the resurrection of the dead. "If only it were true!" The thought of it overwhelms him and his heart faints within him (v. 27c). If there is a continuance of life after this one, then it is even possible for an innocent sufferer, who goes to the grave with no relief whatsoever, to have some hope of vindication.

"God will judge you counselors" (19:28-29)

Though, once again, the meaning is not as clear as we would like, Job appears to be closing his speech with a word of warning to the counselors. They had better be aware that God will judge them for the way they have been treating him. They will be held accountable. What Job suggests here comes to pass in 42:7-9.

Zophar (Chapter 20)

In his first speech (Chap. 11), Zophar had reiterated the doctrine of retribution, suggested that Job probably deserves even worse than he is getting (11:6b), talked at some length about the inability of human beings to understand the mysteries of God, and concluded with an exhortation for Job to repent so that life might again take an upswing for him. In his second speech, Zophar adds nothing to what Eliphaz and Bildad have already said about the ultimate fate of the wicked.

"The exulting of the wicked is short" (20:1-29)

In this second cycle, all three of the counselors are preoccupied with the certainty that wicked people will finally be punished. A typical complaint of a sufferer is that "people more wicked than I are having a good life, and that is not just." Though Job has not been speaking about this, the counselors seem to anticipate Job's comments which we will read in the next chapter.

After a brief mention of his agitation and dissatisfaction with Job's remarks (vv. 1-3), Zophar gets right to the point. Since the beginning of time, it has been true that the "exulting of the wicked is short" (vv. 4-5). From our immediate perspective, it may seem that they are escaping punishment. Though they may look as though they are high and mighty and invulnerable to justice, they will be brought low and perish. Zophar goes on, with great relish, to describe the calamities that will eventually befall the once proud evildoer who is now brought to account with fitting retribution. Again, we should note the apparent delight that inspires the rhetoric of good religious folks as they contemplate the suffering which will be unleashed against the wicked ones who seemed for a time to elude God's scrutiny.

Though this passage could very well be contemplating the fate of individual wicked people, it is interesting to think about this chapter in the context of the exilic period. During those terrible years, many of the followers of the Hebrew God wondered why Babylon was so prosperous while Israel, God's chosen people, had been virtually wiped out. The prophets and historians of Israel had interpreted the disaster as the result of the people's sin, just as Eliphaz and the others insisted that Job must have committed some awful act to merit such punishment. But others began to wonder whether the doctrine of retribution was sufficient to explain the exile. "It may be true that we are disobedient and often faithless followers of God, but compared to the Babylonians, we really look pretty good" (see, for example, Hab. 1:12-17). In response to this concern, prophets and others spoke of the fate which lay in store for Babylon. Though this great nation seemed to be invincible, at the peak of its power and unanswerable to any earthly or heavenly court, nevertheless there will be a judgment and Babylon will have to pay for its excesses against Judah. Some of the words of Zophar in this chapter (e.g., vv. 4-5 and 18-19) could reflect this need to believe in the ultimate downfall of Babylon. Neither wicked persons nor wicked nations should go unpunished or there would be severe doubt about God's desire, ability, or power to execute justice in this world.

Job's Response (Chapter 21)

"Listen and understand my impatience" (21:1-6)

Job begins with a word of advice to his counselors. It is a word that all who attempt to bring consolation to the sufferer should heed. "Listen. That is all I ask. Don't worry about giving answers. Only pay attention to what I am saying. If you can do that, I do not expect anything more from you." Job, at this stage of the game, probably does not expect his exhortation (in v. 2) to do much good, so there is a touch of sarcasm in his suggestion that after he has finished speaking they can proceed to mock him and his words (v. 3).

Job again reminds his friends that his dispute is not with human beings (v. 4a), but rather with God. If they would get out of the way, quit defending God and joining battle against Job, perhaps the quarrel with God could be settled much more quickly. Rather than helping Job resolve the crisis in his relationship with God, they are confusing and complicating the matter by injecting themselves and their own ideas and feelings of self worth into what should be a private conflict between God and Job. If they really stopped to look at Job with unprejudiced eyes, they would see clearly why he is so impatient (v. 4b) and they would be so appalled that they would be speechless (v. 5). They could then no longer be so overconfident in their presumptuous pronouncements about the cause of suffering and the certainty of God's justice for both the innocent and the guilty.

"Why do the wicked prosper?" (21:7-13)

Here, in the final speech of the second cycle, Job is responding to all three of his counselors. All of them have been claiming that, evidence to the contrary, evil people will be punished sooner or later. Job had resisted getting into this argument after Eliphaz, and then Bildad introduced it. Now he replies with complete skepticism toward their naive faith in the inevitability of justice for the wicked.

Look at the wicked. They live to a ripe old age. They are the ones who have the power in the world (v. 7). Their children grow up, take their place in the world, and provide their wicked parents the satisfaction of leaving descendants to carry on when they are gone (v. 8). Everything they do prospers. Their animals reproduce and add to their wealth (v. 10). There is happiness and joy all their life and they go to their death in peace (vv. 11-13). Job paints a lovely picture of the happy and long life of wicked people—a sharp contrast to the prospects presented by Zophar in Chap. 20.

"What's in it for me if I serve God?" (21:14-16)

The wicked are wise about the world—much wiser than most religious people, who seem unwilling to see the world as it really is. Evildoers have observed how the system works and know that they can do what they want without having to answer to God. So they tell God to get lost (v. 14). They don't need to concern themselves with God's will for their lives (v. 14b). There is no profit in serving God, and, since there is nothing to be gained, why do it (v. 15)? They have no fear of retribution. Promises of reward or threats of punishment have no effect in motivating their ethical decisions. They do what they want to get what they want because they see no evidence that God is going to interfere.

This cynical response on the part of the wicked reminds us again of the use of the doctrine of retribution to motivate people to proper ethical action. If it is true that human beings always act out of self-interest, and if the idea of reward and punishment for our actions is lost, then no one will serve God anymore. In their first conversation (1:9-11), Satan had put this possibility before God, and God was then moved to allow the suffering of Job to test Satan's thesis.

In his next speech (22:17-18), Eliphaz will quote the arrogant wicked person in almost the same words used by Job in this section. But Eliphaz will continue to argue that the fate of the wicked is sealed and they will, in fact, be brought to account.

"The wicked will not be punished" (21:17-26)

If his counselors will only look, they will see that there are precious few examples of God punishing the wicked (vv. 17-18). One way of dealing with this problem for Job's friends has been to suggest that even though the sinner is not punished, at least his children will have to pay (v. 19a). That is, God's justice will be administered, alright, but not till the next generation. Job finds this less than adequate justice. What do they care if their children suffer after they are gone, as long as they themselves have a long and prosperous life? If the doctrine of retribution is to make any sense, then the person who sins must be the one to suffer, not those who are born later (vv. 19b-21). (See Ezekiel 18 for a discussion of the problem of the sins of the fathers being passed on to the next generation. Ezekiel says that everyone must pay for his or her own sin.)

Death is the great equalizer. Some people have a good life, long and prosperous, culminating in a peaceful death (vv. 23-24). Others experience nothing but unhappiness and bitterness throughout their whole life (v. 25). But when life is over, they are all in the same situation, lying in the dust and being eaten by worms. This word from Job implies that there is no judgment after death. Not only is it true that the wicked are not punished by God in this life, it is further stated that they will not be subject to retribution in the next world either. For Job, there is no next world. What happens between birth and death is all that there is. After death there is nothing—neither overdue rewards for innocent sufferers nor a final comeuppance for defiant sinners. There is no life beyond this one to rectify the injustices that ought to be obvious to anyone who has looked.

"Well traveled observers know I am right" (21:27-34)

Eliphaz, particularly, had prided himself on his observations of the world. "Think now, who that was innocent ever perished? Or where were the upright cut off?" (4:7). "Lo, this we have searched out; it is true. Hear, and know it is for your good" (5:27). So there is a cutting edge to Job's question, "Have you not asked those who travel the roads, and do you not accept their testimony?" (v. 29). "Talk to people who know something, who have been around, who are not locked in an ivory tower. If you listen to what they tell you, it will become apparent that I am right." The wicked man always seems to escape (v. 30). No one pays him back for what he has done (v. 31). He is even honored after death with a well-attended funeral and a beautiful resting place (vv. 32-33).

The second cycle ends with Job's declaration that all his friends' answers are lies (v. 34). Therefore, there is no comfort in them. No matter what explanation one presents for the presence of suffering, if it is false, it is no help. Perhaps a sufferer could find comfort in the idea that God will eventually work justice, that even the prospering of those "more wicked than I" will come to an end. But if that is only wishful thinking, if it does not stand the test of careful scrutiny, if the data do not support the conclusions, then it is not a word capable of bringing consolation.

B. THE THIRD CYCLE (JOB 22–27)

Eliphaz (Chapter 22)

Eliphaz is again the first one to speak. The content of his message does not change very much from one cycle to the next, but the harshness of his approach to Job steadily increases. This time, Eliphaz will be quite blunt and very specific in articulating Job's sins.

"Does God need human obedience?" (22:1-4)

Job had implied on several occasions that God has some need to preoccupy himself with human beings. God treats Job as if he were a threat, like the ancient sea dragon whom God keeps under control (7:12). Why does God make so much of human beings and spend so much time fretting about how they behave (7:17-18)? Job says, "If I sin, what do I do to thee, thou watcher of men?" (7:20a). Job wants God to let him alone and get off his back (10:20; 14:1-6).

Eliphaz sees this kind of theologizing as too presumptuous. It makes humans more important than they are by proposing that what people do can have an effect on God. It assumes human ability to control the way God thinks and feels. God is so distant and high above mere mortals that it is the worst kind of audacious pride to believe that God is all that concerned or moved by what we do. We cannot do anything to profit God (v. 2). God does not get any pleasure if we are righteous (v. 3) nor (to state the opposite) is God particularly displeased if we are disobedient. The world operates like clockwork. The doctrine of retribution is not for the benefit of God but for a human's own good. God's "feelings" do not enter into the picture at all.

Is God coldly removed from the pain and sin and joy of God's human creatures, as Eliphaz suggests? Though there may be a valid theological point

here, Eliphaz, to say the least, has pushed it too far and has ignored many
dominant biblical themes about God. God does care what humans do and
how they feel. In Chaps. 1 and 2, God seems to need assurance that Job's
devotion can survive the loss of his good fortune. God is often angry about
the way we treat each other. God is sorrowful when we turn away from him
and follow other gods. God is moved to action by the cries of his children
in distress. God often "repents" of evil that he had intended to bring as
punishment because God cannot bear to destroy those whom he loves (see
Hosea 11, for example). God takes great delight in every individual sinner
who repents (see Luke 15). And God even cares enough to suffer with us on
the cross. This is hardly the picture of a cold, indifferent, immovable, un-
feeling God that Eliphaz lays before Job.[21]

Eliphaz, in each of his three presentations, has talked about the low estate
of the human race in relationship to God. Human beings cannot be righteous
before God and God, who cannot even trust the angels, certainly has no
confidence in mere mortals (4:17-19). In the second cycle, Eliphaz returned
to this theme and repeated that humans can never be clean or trustworthy
(15:14-16). Now the same negative words about humanity appear again in
the third speech. On this, Eliphaz is consistent.

"You are a wicked person, Job" (22:5-11)

Eliphaz finally comes right out and says it. "There is no end to your
iniquities" (v. 5b). The doctrine of retribution works. Job is a sinner. It all
makes sense. In Chaps. 4–5, Eliphaz had been gentle, apparently troubled
by Job's plight and the incongruity when a good man like Job has to suffer
so much. But Eliphaz had changed his mind about Job over the course of the
discussion. The words of Job must have had a powerful effect in moving
Eliphaz into the outright condemnations that we see in this passage.

Eliphaz goes on to recite specific sins which Job has committed (vv. 6-
9). It is a stereotyped list of offenses against the poor, the naked, the thirsty,
the hungry, the powerless, the widows, and the orphans. To commit these
crimes is to go against the traditions of the law codes and the prophets. One
is reminded of Jesus' condemnation of the goats in Matt. 25:41-46.

Even if Eliphaz here were speaking the truth, we might question his
pastoral style. The confrontation seems cruel and inappropriate. But, in this
case, Eliphaz has done even worse because it is almost certain that he speaks
lies about Job. His condemnation is based on his doctrine of retribution that
must find a sin to justify the punishment rather than on actual observance of
the way Job has lived. In Chaps. 1 and 2 we were told, by God himself, that
Job was blameless and upright (1:8 and 2:3). In Chap. 31, Job recalls the

high ethical standards which he had always maintained, in direct contrast to the picture presented here by Eliphaz. Whom should we believe—God and Job, or Eliphaz?

"God will see and judge the wicked" (22:12-20)

Again, the subject of the ultimate fate of the wicked is presented. This time it is quite clear that Eliphaz associates Job with the evildoers about whom he is speaking. To be sure, God lives high in the heavens (v. 12) but wicked people (like Job) then come to the mistaken conclusion that God does not know what they are doing (v. 13), as if the thick clouds that surround God prevent God from seeing what is happening on earth (vv. 13b-14). Those who have been led astray by this way of thinking in the past have been punished (v. 16), even though they had deluded themselves by arrogantly telling God to "get lost" and had believed that they were immune from any retaliation (v. 17). This verse is very similar to Job's quote of the wicked in 21:14-15. Job said that the wicked can get away with such thinking because God does not, in fact, act to punish the guilty. Eliphaz turns the quote around to make it sound like a sentiment that Job himself uses as an excuse to justify his own unethical behavior. Job wishes that God would punish the wicked, but does not see that it is happening. Eliphaz maintains that God does punish the wicked; therefore, people like Job who think that such judgment does not take place should beware.

"Return to God and all will be well" (22:21-30)

This theme has been heard from Eliphaz before (e.g., 5:17ff.). If Job will return to God, make peace (v. 21), accept God's teaching (v. 22), humble himself (v. 23a), and remove unrighteousness from his house (v. 23b), then prosperity will return. Job will delight himself in the Almighty (v. 26), his prayers will be answered (v. 27), and whatever he undertakes will be successful (v. 28). With this optimism about how "everything will come out all right," Eliphaz probably would have done well on American television. "Turn to God and repent, accept my teachings about God, and you too can be relieved of all your miseries and may even accumulate some material rewards for your righteousness."

The reference to gold in vv. 24-25 is not clear. It seems unlikely that Eliphaz is telling Job to throw away his gold and let God be his treasure. Job has already lost everything. He has no gold in which to put his trust. Perhaps the intention is to counsel Job to stop worrying about what he has lost and realize that true and lasting riches are present in our relationship with God. Therefore, even though we are poor, as the world measures such things, we are still wealthy because of our faith in God. Or (and this may be the most likely in the light of what we know about Eliphaz) perhaps Eliphaz is promising Job that he will return to prosperity (e.g., v. 28) and he will have so much gold that it will be as common for him as dust or the stones in a stream (v. 24).[22]

Once more it has been assumed that Job's suffering is his own fault. The only hurdle that stands between him and a glorious and affluent future is his inability or unwillingness to face up to his own faults and return to God with proper humility. In his present situation, that is not a helpful word for Job.

Job's Response (Chapters 23 and 24)

"Where can I find God to make my case?" (23:1-9)

This passage contains poignant words of a sufferer who has lost a sense of God's presence "Oh, that I knew where I might find him" (v. 3a). Where do you turn when you are convinced that only God can help you (human beings have failed you), but you do not know where to find God (vv. 3a, 8-9), and, if you should somehow make connections with the elusive deity, you are not altogether certain what kind of reception you will get (vv. 4-7)? Job is still thinking in courtroom imagery. He wants to make his case before God and he hopes for an acquittal. All along, he has been contending that he is innocent, that he does not deserve his suffering. Perhaps God has somehow let this case slip by without knowing all the facts and Job wants the opportunity to clarify his position. Or, maybe there is really something that God knows about a secret sin of which even Job is unaware. If this should be the situation, then the accusation should be out in the open so that Job can deal with it. Either way, Job wants a word with God.

Job expects to get a fair hearing. Though he has been saying things which indicate a lack of confidence in God's justice, here (vv. 5-7) he talks as if he will be heard and not simply overwhelmed by God's power. As we shall note later, when Job finally gets his confrontation with God (beginning in Chap. 38), God will do all the talking, Job will not be permitted to "make his case," and God most certainly will "contend with Job in the greatness of his power" (v. 6a).

Job has a problem in his persistence in hanging on to the doctrine of retribution, his inability to shake the imagery of the courtroom as a metaphor for the way God relates to human beings. Therefore, when God finally responds to Job, it will not be on this juridical level at all. God will refuse to deal with Job as a court case, with indictments, evidence presented, and the judgment of guilt or innocence.

"If tried fairly, I'll come out OK" (23:10-12)

Once again Job reveals that he still expects that the world should run according to the doctrine of retribution. God knows what a good person Job has been, how he has never turned aside from God's way (v. 11) nor departed from God's commandments (v. 12). The outcome of the trial ought to be a foregone conclusion. Job should come forth like pure gold (v. 10). If God had been running the world according to the rules, none of this should have happened to Job in the first place.

"God does what he wants and I'm terrified" (23:13-17)

Job's first problem is simply where to find God. How do you locate God? How do you make an appointment with the Almighty? Since God cannot be seen and is seldom heard, where do you go to seek some certainty from God in a world of confusion and uncertainty? Even if Job should somehow gain an audience with the Creator of the universe, can he stand up and argue with the One who has all the cards, who both writes the rules and then interprets them? Earlier in the chapter, Job had spoken with confidence about having a fair hearing (vv. 5-7), but now Job seems not so sure about that. Job believes that he *should* be acquitted, but what if God has already decided and will not change (vv. 13-14)? Human beings cannot make God do anything. God does what God wants. If Job can no longer count on the doctrine of retribution, on a moral God who acts with perceptible justice toward the world, then Job is indeed terrified (v. 15). Nothing is certain. He is completely at the mercy of an arbitrary and capricious and unreliable power against which no human can contend. (Job had earlier, in Chap. 9, for example, raised questions about how mere mortals can argue with God.)

There is much ambivalence in Job's search for a God who will judge his case. He wants that judgment and yet he doesn't. He still trusts God and yet he doesn't. He loves God and yet he is terrified of God. But, when all is said and done, there is no place else to turn.

"Why doesn't God punish the wicked?" (24:1-17)

The arguments about whether or not the wicked will ever be punished continue. It is becoming rather monotonous and a bit tedious. Every speaker is very predictable. If the counselors are talking, you expect them to defend God's justice and state with utmost confidence that God will take care of those nasty people sooner or later. If Job is speaking, we expect to hear a critique of God's justice in allowing wickedness to go unpunished while the victims of injustice cry out to God in vain. That is exactly what we read in this passage.

Wicked people take away the animals (v. 3) and land (v. 4) of the orphans and widows, and even take poor children as slaves (v. 9). This leaves the oppressed in a terrible plight, forced to forage and glean in someone else's field to provide food for their children (vv. 5-6), naked and without shelter from the elements (vv. 7-8), and, ironically, they work the wine presses but are denied a taste of wine to quench their own thirst (v. 11). But when these powerless and persecuted members of society cry out to God for help, "God pays no attention to their prayer" (v. 12b). As long as God takes no action to relieve the burden, to punish the wicked—at least to make them stop doing what they are doing—there will be no justice for the poor.

The wicked love the darkness and fear the light (vv. 13-17). They will continue in their evil ways as long as they can escape notice so that no one (not even God) will bring them to account.

"(You say) 'God will punish them' " (24:18-25)

These next few verses have stirred up considerable discussion among Job scholars. As the text presently stands, Job is the speaker. He has just finished telling his friends that God does not act to save the needy and punish their tormentors. That is a consistent word from Job. But in this section, the opposite is stated. The wicked will be wiped out by disasters. Justice works, after all. This sounds more like the counselors than Job. After being exalted a little while, they shall wither and be cut off (v. 24). Perhaps Job could have spoken vv. 21-23 and v. 25, but it is more likely that what we have here is actually a speech by one of the counselors, now—for some reason—assigned to Job. The RSV prefaces v. 18 with "You say. . .," which implies that Job is quoting his friends and not speaking his own words. In this way the entire speech is kept in Job's mouth. But there is nothing in the Hebrew text like the words "You say. . . . " This is only a speculation to try to make sense out of the confusion.

Most scholars think that 24:18-25 is actually part of Zophar's third speech (another part could be 27:13-23). As the book of Job presently stands, Zophar does not speak in the third cycle of speeches. Perhaps what was originally ascribed to him has now been put in the mouth of Job. But why would someone juggle and rearrange the speeches of the counselors and Job? A possible explanation would be that a pious editor, bothered by Job's statement of God's indifference to the suffering of the oppressed (e.g., 24:12) could not resist the urge to make Job a bit more orthodox by having him come out for eventual justice on God's part. "They are exalted a little while, and then are gone" (v. 24a).[23]

We shall need to say more about the problem of who is actually speaking in some of these speeches at the end of the third cycle.

Bildad (Chapter 25)

"Humans cannot be righteous before God" (25:1-6)

This is a very short speech from Bildad. The whole chapter is only six verses long; then Job speaks again in Chap. 26. Some scholars suggest that 26:5-14 may be a continuation of this speech by Bildad. We shall discuss this possibility later. At any rate, there is little doubt that Chap. 25 belongs to one of Job's counselors and no reason to assign it to anyone other than Bildad himself.

This is not the first time that Job's friends have spoken about the low estate of human beings as compared to God. No human is righteous in God's eyes (v. 4). If even the heavenly bodies, the moon and stars, are not clean in God's eyes (v. 5), then how can a human, a maggot, a worm, have the audacity to claim innocence in the presence of God Almighty (v. 6)? Bildad professes a "worm theology," with a vengeance.

Eliphaz had expressed such sentiments in 4:17-21; 15:14-16; and 22:1-4. Zophar, too, spoke disparagingly of worthless human beings in 11:5-12. Even Job admitted that human beings are not in the same league with God as far as wisdom and power are concerned (as in 9:2-12; 12:9-25; and 14:4). But Job is not willing to abandon integrity and accept a doctrine of general human perversion in order to make God look better in the dispute that is going on between them. As God's justice comes increasingly under attack, defenders of God tend to speak louder and louder about the depravity of people. Someone must be at fault for the troubles of the world. It can't be God, because God wouldn't act like that. Then it must be human beings. And if humans appear to be good and undeserving of such punishment, then we must probe deeper and point out that no one is righteous, everyone is a sinner, and, as a proper and justifiable consequence of sinful nature, no one is immune to suffering.

Job probably did not believe in the total depravity of human beings. Perhaps his counselors did hold to such a belief, as a way of assigning blame even when seemingly innocent persons suffer.

Job's Response (Chapters 26 and 27, or Parts Thereof)

If Job always takes the position that God does not properly punish the wicked, and if Job's friends always push for the inevitability of God's justice, then we have some problems in these two chapters. There is nothing in our text to indicate that anyone other than Job is speaking. He is mentioned at the beginning of Chap. 26 and again at the top of Chap. 27, with no intervening speech by anyone else. And yet the words that are uttered sometimes sound like Job and sometimes sound like the others. Further, Zophar has no speech ascribed to him in the third cycle and Bildad's is very short. All of this has led to an enormous amount of speculation, with a great diversity of conclusions, with regard to the identity of the speaker and the order of the speeches in these two chapters.[24] We will return to this discussion later in this chapter.

"How you have helped the powerless!" (26:1-4)

Job begins by saying, "How you have helped him who has no power! How you have saved the arm that has no strength!" (v. 2). We are immediately faced with an important question of interpretation. Who is this weak person whom Bildad and the others have "helped"? Is it Job talking about himself in a way meant to mock their inability to bring comfort to one who suffers? Or is Job talking about God? Bildad has just been talking (in Chap. 25) about the greatness of God as contrasted with the miserable state of humanity. Is Job perhaps, in words dripping with irony and sarcasm, ridiculing the efforts of Bildad and company to defend the Almighty God from the bitter and despairing assaults of suffering human beings? Already in Chap. 13, Job had protested that his friends always took God's side, showing partiality toward God (13:10), even telling lies in order to make God look good and Job look bad (13:7-8). It is certainly ironic to think of puny mortals (described as "worms" by Bildad in 25:6) rushing in to save God, who "has no power" or whose "arm has no strength." The message from Job to his intended comforters is that they should step back and see how silly it has been to defend the One who needs no defense. It would have been much better if they had come to Job's defense, because he was the one who *really* has no power.

So, is Job talking about himself in vv. 2-3, or is he talking about God? Either way, this is a devastating critique of the way his friends have failed him. They have not comforted him and God certainly does not need to be defended by the likes of them.

Some students of the book of Job have even ascribed these words to Bildad and have read them as directed against Job. (See Eliphaz's reference to Job as a counselor in 4:3-4.) This would be a sarcastic put-down of Job, his pretentiousness, his windy words which disturb the piety of the faithful.

I do not think this last interpretation is correct. It is not easy to decide between the other two, and maybe it is not necessary to do so. I am attracted to the heavy sarcasm implied in the idea of humans rallying around in defense of a God who cannot help himself.

"God is the creator of all" (26:5-14)

This is a lovely little hymn extolling the power of God in creation, emphasizing God's dominion even over Sheol (vv. 5-6) and God's power to control the forces of chaos, here represented by Rahab, the fleeing serpent (vv. 12-13).

Again, most commentators raise the question of who is speaking. The most common conclusion is to assign these verses to Bildad. They follow, with some logic, after 25:6, further expanding the theme of the power and majesty of God. This, then, would be part of Bildad's third speech, though, for some reason it has now been divided by the words of Job in 26:1-4.

Of course, these words could have been spoken by Job himself. Job knows about the power of God and has at times spoken of God in words not dissimilar to these (e.g., 9:1-13). But many have thought that such words from Job would not be expected in this context, when he has been protesting God's failure to execute justice in the world rather than God's power over the world.[25]

If Job in 26:2-3 was actually referring to God as the "powerless" one whom the counselors were so eager to "help," then maybe this little hymn to God's power would be appropriate in the mouth of Job. It would be a way of emphasizing the power of God and highlighting the preposterous pretension of mortals who feel the need to come to the aid of a God like that. This "powerless" God that they are so frantic to help is actually the one who supervises Sheol, moves the heavenly bodies around, sets up boundaries between light and darkness, and smites the primeval sea monster. The sense of irony is heightened if this passage is seen in this context.

"I will uphold my integrity" (27:1-6)

This has the look of a concluding statement on the part of Job. In v. 2, Job takes an oath, swearing by God that he will not speak falsehood (v. 4) by saying that his friends are right in their condemnation of him (v. 5) or by giving up his claim to be righteous (v. 6). He cannot believe that he is a bad person deserving of his suffering, and nothing that anyone has said has changed his mind. Therefore, he must take his stand on what he knows about himself, on his own integrity, no matter what God or humans say about him.

It is interesting that Job swears an oath in the name of the same God whom he accuses of "taking away his right" and "making his soul bitter" (v. 2). Here, again, we see how Job is torn back and forth between two views of God. On the one hand, God is the powerful controller of all that happens in the world and is therefore responsible in a direct way for all of Job's misfortunes. On the other hand, God is the loving Creator with whom Job once had a warm relationship, a moral force who governs the universe with fairness, and therefore one who can be approached with the hope of receiving justice and compassion and vindication.

"What is the hope of the godless?" (27:7-12)

Is Job speaking here or is this one of the counselors? Again, we have some uncertainty. Verses 7-10 seem to indicate that there is no hope for the godless. They will be cut off by God who (it is implied) will not respond to their cry in times of trouble (v. 9). The confident expectation of justice against the wicked sounds more like the counselors than Job. The claim to speak an authentic word from God (v. 11) as over against the vain words of others (v. 12) sounds like something that either Job or the counselors might say to each other. There is no reticence to proclaim truth for one's own positions and folly for one's opponents on the part of any of the participants in this lengthy dialog that is now—mercifully—drawing to a close.

"The prosperity of the wicked man will soon vanish" (27:13-23)

It is very unlikely that this is a word from Job. If it is Job, it would have to be sarcasm, tongue-in-cheek wishful thinking. Since it appears in a section ascribed to Job (at least no other names are given), perhaps it shows an editor's efforts to make Job more orthodox and confident in the eventuality of God's judgment on the wicked. Many commentators ascribe this passage to Zophar's third speech (which may also include 27:7-12 and 24:18-25).

So we end the third cycle in a considerable amount of confusion about who is speaking, and feeling somewhat bored with endless discussion of what will finally happen to bad people. At this point, one might wonder where the discussion can go from here. There has certainly been nothing new said by anyone for a long, long time.

C. SIGNIFICANT THEOLOGICAL, PASTORAL, AND INTERPRETIVE POINTS RAISED BY CHAPTERS 15–27

Before moving on through the book of Job, let us pause to glimpse an overview of some important considerations raised by the various speakers during the second and third cycles.

1. The punishment of wicked people

The discussion of the fate of the wicked dominates the second and third cycles. Why are Job and his counselors so preoccupied with this subject? Why are religious people often absorbed in such questions? Proponents of *the* true religion, *the* acceptable moral code, or *the* definitive catechism usually find themselves speculating about the fate of those who disagree with such God-given absolutes. What will happen to the wicked? If they don't get punished within this life, surely they will get their retribution in hell. We religious people love to theorize about who is saved and who is not, about who will make it to heaven and who will surely be sent to the other place.

If God is a God of justice, then wickedness must be punished. We need to have a sense of order. We need to believe in a God who acts in a sensible, orderly, moral, and just way. Therefore, innocent people must not suffer and wicked people need to be punished. As mentioned earlier, many fear that all ethical motivation will be lost if the wicked are not punished. There will be no restraint on their compulsion to carry out their evil activities.

There are a few reasons why we should pause a moment as we think about this subject. There is a considerable amount of hostility involved in the discussion of the fate of the wicked ones. It is rather unseemly for religious people, particularly those who have been exhorted to love their enemies, to find pleasure in the suffering of others (even though they be sinners), or to feel unhappiness in their prosperity. Probably very few of us ever achieve the magnanimity to rejoice in the well-being of those whom we hate, but we should at least be a little bothered by our passionate desire for their undoing.

We are told, and we believe, that God loves sinners. God then must love those persons whom we judge to be worthy of the most severe punishment. Do we intend to limit God's mercy by demanding that God must punish? Who are we to say that God must act with complete logic, repaying tit for tat, giving the exact wage due and not indulging the late arrival in the vineyard who put in only one hour's work? Must God work according to our standards of justice when perhaps God prefers to act with mercy and compassion? We have imposed our needs for justice, our favorable evaluation of ourselves as over against others, on God. Sometimes God surprises—by sending Jonah to bring the Assyrians to repentance, or by sending his Son to preach acceptance to prostitutes and tax collectors. Religious people don't like it. God does not act according to God's own rules. Nothing is certain any more. "What good does it do me to sacrifice and work like a dog to keep the commandments when the wicked people get just as good a deal, or better, than what I get?"

Probably the prosperity of the wicked is a much bigger problem for us religious people than it is for God.

2. God's control over all that happens

Job never wavered in his belief that everything that happens is God's will. God must have the power to do what God wants. That's what it means to be God. So, God is directly responsible for all the disasters that came to Job. Even when Job complains about humans who have turned away from him and hurt him, he still puts the primary responsibility on God (e.g., 19:13-19). "Nothing happens in this world unless God causes it," thinks Job.

Many people think as Job. If they believe in God at all, they tend to assume that God has power and control over events which take place. When disasters come to people, they often respond, sometimes even without thinking, by saying that "It must be God's will." If God is not in charge, then what good is God?

People want a God who is both all-powerful and just. As long as life goes along well for us, it is relatively easy to believe in both. At times of suffering, especially when the innocent appear to be the ones who are in pain, it becomes more difficult to keep both these desired attributes of God in balance. If God is just, then why doesn't God use God's power to right the wrong? If God is all-powerful, why doesn't a sense of justice compel God to use God's power?

Job was having a hard time maintaining a sense of both omnipotence and justice in God. One of them began to slip. Since Job continued to see God as the all-powerful one, that meant that Job began to doubt God's justice. Job's counselors, on the other hand, were able to keep both omnipotence and justice in their view of God, but they had to imagine sins on the part of Job and the inevitability of punishment for the wicked in this life in order to make it work.

If you must give up a little of either power or justice with regard to God, which would be more helpful to retain? If you cannot have both, which is the easier to let go? Most nonsuffering observers, like Job's counselors, will work hard to keep both in balance and not be forced to make a choice. But for sufferers, like Job, it is often more comforting to back off a little from God's absolute control for the sake of continuing to believe in a God who is just, loving, merciful, and caring. A sufferer may prefer *not* to name God as the cause of suffering, to affirm that God does *not* do things to hurt people, to allow that some things happen in this world that God does not like any more than we do. Whether it is because of human sin or the work of the devil or just plain bad luck or some great mystery, my suffering may not be what God wills at all. God is not my adversary, as Job thought, because God did not bring my suffering. Rather, wherever it came from, God suffers with me and will not leave me without comfort and some hope for an end to the pain.

One of Job's problems, making his torment much more acute, was his belief that God had caused his trouble (especially in Chaps. 16 and 19). If he had been able to relax a little in his insistence on God's complete control over all that happens, perhaps he would have had less doubts about God's justice.

3. The need for vindication of one's name

Job's suffering was compounded by the loss of respect which accompanied his misfortune. It was bad enough to lose property, family, and health, but on top of that he knew that he was considered to be responsible for his own trouble. Those who used to treat him with honor and dignity now raise their eyebrows and imagine what kind of a sinner he must have been to end up like this. When he was dead and gone he would be remembered as a pitiful wretch whom God had punished, rather than a wise man who gave counsel to others and was honored as a pillar of the community.

It is important to us to be remembered well, to be regarded highly by our children and grandchildren. There is a kind of immortality in leaving behind a good reputation, a complimentary epitaph on our tombstone. We occasionally read stories in the newspaper about a person who is trying to restore the good name of a great-grandfather, long dead, who was unjustly convicted of a crime.

So it was with Job. He did not have much to hope for in his devastated life. He expected to die without regaining health. He had no firm belief in any life beyond this one. He hoped that someone at least would redeem his name, whether it be God or another human being, so that future generations would know that he was an innocent sufferer. No matter what the counselors and others said about him, he hoped that he would some day be vindicated, that the world would again think well of him.

That hope is still important. The certainty that one will be well remembered can be a great comfort at the time of facing death.

4. The silence of God

God is silent for many people much of the time. We do not receive telephone calls or special delivery letters from the Almighty. Seldom do we hear a divine voice telling us what to do or giving meaning to events in our lives. We look for a word from God in the Scripture, or a sermon, or the advice of a good friend. Or perhaps we ask God to give us a sign. Because we seldom hear God directly we try to figure out "what God is telling us" by interpreting what our life experiences mean. When disasters come one after another, as with Job, we are bewildered by what God might be saying through all of this.

So Job, as all of us in similar situations, wants a word with God. He wants to know why this is happening to him, what God has in mind, how it can be stopped and a good life resumed. But where do you look for God? If God does not speak, and the usual ways of hearing God (Scripture, religious tradition, advice of friends, interpreting events) are not providing any answers, then where do you go? Job looked everywhere for God (especially note 23:3, 8-9), but God was nowhere to be found. There is nothing that he can do. You cannot control God. You cannot make God step out of the silence and speak. You cannot pick yourself up by your own bootstraps and concoct a religious experience of certainty and "blessed assurance." Maybe God is speaking all the time and we simply cannot hear. Maybe God's silence is more our problem of shutting him out than his deliberate hesitation to converse with us. But for the sufferer, it all seems the same. When one most needs a word from God, that word is not heard. It will come, as we will see later on in Job. The silence will not last forever. In the meantime, it can be terrible and lonely and frightening until God speaks and we recognize the voice.

5. Why the confusion at the end of the third cycle?

The third cycle of speeches finally becomes mired in a discussion of the fate of the wicked in which we are never sure who is speaking. Though Job is identified as the speaker at times, the words seem those of the counselors. What is going on? Why such a mess?

Maybe we should simply read the text as it stands and assume that Job is saying all the words ascribed to him. If so, then Job must change his mind from earlier speeches—which seems very unlikely, especially in the light of some things he will say later on in Chaps. 29 to 31. Or perhaps Job is derisively quoting some of the things said by his counselors. You would have to *hear* Job say it to catch the tone of voice, the tongue-in-cheek, the subtle sarcasm which does not come through in the written word.

Maybe the text was changed accidentally by scribes who were careless in their copying so that pages were placed out of order, resulting in confusion about who was speaking and when. Though that may be possible, it is hard to believe that the present order of the text and identification of speakers is meaningless. One would think that the scribes probably read what they copied and would have recognized the inconsistencies on the part of Job and would have tried to straighten out the material so that it would make better sense.

Perhaps the confusion is deliberate—either by the author or by later editors. If by the author, there might be some point that he is trying to make in the way this part of the book ends. How should he end the discussion between Job and his friends? It has been going nowhere for some time now. No one is listening to anyone else. They have long ago forgotten about Job and his problems and are now abstractly talking about the fate of hypothetical wicked people. It really doesn't matter who is speaking, because no one is listening. The arguments are futile. Intellectualizing about suffering has become a tedious and fruitless business, no matter who is talking or what they are saying. Perhaps the author is trying to convey something of this mood by the form of the final cycle, with its endless repetition and confusion about who is speaking. Not many scholars would support this conclusion, but it is worth contemplating.

Many students of Job conclude that the confusion is deliberate on the part of later editors who were bothered by Job's complete skepticism concerning God's ultimate judgment on the wicked. Therefore they try to get Job to say some things at the end which are more in harmony with an optimistic, orthodox position. Thus, Job finally begins to sound like his counselors.

6. Hope for life after death

Does the book of Job ever come forward with a clear hope for continued life beyond the grave? We looked at this question after discussing the first cycle, and we should pause to see what has been added in the second and third cycles. At the very best, there is some ambiguity. In 17:11-16 Job looks ahead to his own death in words which hold little hope for a new life when this one is over. In 21:26, Job points out that we all come to a common end, lying in the dust and covered with worms, whether we have had a prosperous life or a bitter one. The implication is that there is no judgment following this life, no possibility for the wicked (but happy) to be punished or the innocent (but suffering) to be rewarded.

The passage 19:26-27 comes close to a belief in a future life because Job hopes to see God and to know of his vindication. If that does not occur until after his death, then Job will have to come back to life in order to have consciousness of it. This passage (along with some verses in Chap. 14, particularly vv. 7-9,13-17), is about as close as the book of Job ever comes to articulating a belief in life after death. And, in both Chaps. 14 and 19, it is more like an expression of longing and yearning (even "wishful thinking") than a confident assertion that there is more to life than we can see from this side of the grave.

7. Is Job asking about corporate as well as individual suffering?

We read the story of Job as the struggle of an individual innocent sufferer to come to terms with his terrible situation. We identify with Job in our own efforts to find meaning and to maintain faith in God during times of suffering. But Job may also be asking questions about the fate of the people of Judah, the ones chosen by God and promised an eternal relationship with him, who have been virtually destroyed by the invading Babylonians. There are some passages in Job (e.g., 17:1-10; 18:14-21; 19:7-12; and 20:4-5,18-19) which make good sense in the context of the Babylonian exile, when God's people were trying to understand what their suffering meant. Was it punishment, as prophets and historians had said? Was it *only* punishment? Though Judah was certainly sinful (all humans, and all nations are unrighteous in God's eyes, after all), one could argue (as Habakkuk and others did) that there are degrees of sinfulness. Certainly, on any meaningful scale of wickedness, the Babylonians were worse than the Jews, though the Jews were the ones who were suffering. Is God not just? Will any good emerge from all this suffering? Will final vindication ever come? Will the good name of Judah ever be remembered with respect instead of being a "byword" among the nations? Will the wicked (Babylon itself as a primary example) ever be punished?

Many of the questions raised about Job, the individual sufferer, would therefore be the same ones raised about the people as a whole. The book of Job can be read either way, though certainly our tendency is to read it as a story about an individual, not a story about the suffering of Judah. At the least, the time of the exile raised the issue of innocent suffering in a way that would have provided the context for a book like Job, and the language of Job's lamenting at times resembles the language of psalms and lamentations over the destruction of the nation.

8. Job's relationship with his counselors

At the beginning, the counselors came with the desire to bring comfort to Job. They wept with him and were profoundly moved by the horrible things that had happened to him. But somewhere along the way, their view of Job changed and they were no longer able to help him in his torment. The change in Eliphaz is the most dramatic as he moves from a calm and careful teacher of tradition (Chaps. 4–5) to an open accuser of Job (Chap. 22). What went wrong between Job and his ministers?

(*a*) The counselors came to Job with the idea that good is rewarded and evil punished within this life. That meant that they approached Job from the very first with the assumption that there must be something wrong with him. Everything that they said, directly or indirectly, revealed their basic belief that Job was responsible for his own trouble.

(*b*) Job's friends were no doubt relieved at Job's initial response of submission and humility and patience in the face of great adversity (Chaps. 1–

2). He would be easy to counsel—no crying out and complaining and giving up on God and asking embarrassing and impossible questions. The pastor breathes a sigh of relief when the recipient of great suffering "takes it well" and "sets a good example of faith for others."

(c) Job begins to lament in Chap. 3 and we can almost see the counselors tense up. This is not going to be so easy after all. Job wishes he had never been born and wants to die to get out of his misery. "We must talk him out of that kind of negative thinking. We must cheer him up. He might hurt himself. We thought he was a believer but now he is talking like that."

(d) Though Eliphaz led off the discussion with soft words and reasoned explanations for suffering, there was no mistaking a patronizing, and even condemning, undertone to his first speech. Job heard and understood. He felt put down, blamed, insulted, abandoned, and he responded with severe words of judgment on his so-called friends.

(e) From Job's response in Chaps. 6–7, the dialog steadily declined. Job was saying awful things about God and other people. He was hostile toward their efforts at ministry. He was giving himself away. Their doctrine of retribution was verified by the way Job was behaving. He was not such a good person after all. His suffering did make sense, either as punishment or as discipline to bring him to a better awareness of how self-righteous he had been and how great is the gap between God and human beings.

(f) The counselors had closely identified themselves and their message with the person and words of God. An attack on them was an attack on God, and vice versa. They became terribly defensive of God's reputation and their own wisdom and skill as counselors. They let Job get under their skin, make them angry, and turn them aside from their original purpose ("to come to condole with him and comfort him," 2:11). Job and his needs were no longer the center of their attention, but rather their defense of their theories of how God works in the world had become their chief concern.

(g) From Chap. 3, Job had wanted to lament, but his friends wanted to argue theology. They were approaching the question of suffering on two different levels. Job wanted a responsive ear, a friend to hear his lament, the recognition that someone knew and understood how awful it must be for him, permission to go out on a limb and say outlandish words that might verge on blasphemy in order to get some of his pain off his chest. But the counselors, with furrowed brow and pious earnestness, paid too much attention to the words. They responded to the content, not the hurt. They detected the flaws in Job's theology and they began to argue. For a time, Job tries to continue the lament and not enter their discussion, but, finally, he too joins the debate about whether or not the wicked will be punished. He meets them on their level and goes with their agenda.

And so, by the end of the third cycle, Job and his friends are locked in a useless discussion about the fate of the wicked. It looks as though it could go on forever. Something dramatic will need to occur before Job can get out of this rut. That will not happen till Chap. 38.

5

The Conclusion of the Dialogs (Job 28-31)

Eliphaz, Bildad, and Zophar have all had their say. No doubt they have all talked too much already. But this section of the book is not yet finished. Job, who had the first word (Chap. 3), will also have the last word (Chaps. 29–31). Before that, however, we must look at Chap. 28, a poem about the difficulty humans have in acquiring wisdom.

A. THE WISDOM POEM (CHAPTER 28)

Some Introductory Questions

1. Who is speaking in Chap. 28? That is a question that has been widely debated by students of the book of Job. Could it be Job himself? No speaker is mentioned at the beginning of the chapter. The last one to be named is Job, at the beginning of Chap. 27. But there is a broad consensus that Job did not speak the last half of Chap. 27, let alone Chap. 28. There have been a few attempts to see Bildad or Zophar as the speaker, particularly Zophar, who says words somewhat similar to these in 11:7-12 and (as many scholars suppose) in 27:13-23. Though the case for Zophar is stronger than for Bildad, there is little support for ascribing this chapter to either of them (perhaps

because we hesitate to ascribe such lovely words to those clumsy purveyors of religious platitudes).

If the words of Chap. 28 do not fit in the mouths of any of the participants in the drama, perhaps they are the direct words of the author of the book (i.e., the one who wrote the dialogs and God's speeches in 38–41), introduced as an interlude in the conversation. Some have thought so, but have had difficulty explaining why it should be inserted at this particular place. Others have thought it impossible that the author put Chap. 28 here because it would "upstage" God and make the substance of God's speeches unnecessary.[26] According to many, therefore, it must have been placed in this position in the book by someone at a later time, though, again, the reason for its inclusion is still rather difficult to understand.

2. Why is Chap. 28 placed here in the book of Job? Whether or not we can explain its present position, we are given the book of Job as it is. Someone put the poem here for some reason.

It does not seem likely that it is a speech by Job. Perhaps later on, after his encounter with God, Job will be able to agree with the sentiments expressed in this chapter. At that point, he will be willing to recognize the limitations on human reason and to accept that many of his questions will remain unanswered. But the next three chapters find Job still very much preoccupied with the doctrine of retribution and approaching God as if answers to his specific questions are still possible. It is not likely that the serenity and acceptance of human limits in Chap. 28 would be so quickly replaced by the tone and content of Chaps. 29–31.

It does not seem likely that Zophar (who had no third speech) is speaking here. He is, of course, not identified as the speaker. The reader gets the impression that this chapter is a positive expression, a statement of what the author wants to say, rather than (as in previous speeches by the counselors) examples of poor theology or bad pastoral practice which are criticized by Job.

It seems most probable to me that this is a statement by the author, a transition, a time to stop and catch your breath. On the one hand, it points to the futility of the search for answers that has gone on for so many chapters. On the other hand, it points ahead to the climax of the book—when God says words similar to these. My own experience, and that of many of my students, is that Chap. 28 appears as a breath of fresh air, a hint that there might actually be a way out of this endless search for answers. Job may not be ready to hear this word. Surely, he is not ready to say it. His speaking in Chaps. 29–31 reveals how hard it is to give up the search. Maybe Chap. 28 is written for us, the readers. Only later will its truth be accepted by Job himself.

One cannot dismiss Chap. 28 by suggesting that it steals God's lines and makes Chaps. 38–41 unnecessary. This is not the first time that Job (and we) have been told that human beings cannot know all there is to know. As noted, Zophar said that in 11:7-12. If these words are merely another effort to rationalize human suffering, another attempt to find the "answer," they would not be much help to Job. For him, it is insufficient to say that "God knows more than humans and you might as well quit banging your head against the wall trying to answer questions that cannot be answered." Job still hears that word as a rebuke, as a squelching of his freedom to ask the hard questions, as an antiintellectual acceptance of ignorance as a natural state. When humans say such words to each other they are not necessarily "upstaging" God. The difference in Chaps. 38–41 is not in the content but in the fact that God himself is saying these words. It is the relationship with God, the certainty of God's presence, that makes the difference. Now it will no longer be just one more way of trying to explain away suffering. If God reveals himself to me and tells me that I can trust him and do not have to answer all my questions, then I will listen. As long as Bildad or Zophar tell me such things, I will be suspicious that they are trying to protect their own positions from my embarrassing questions.

The Inaccessibility of Wisdom (Chapter 28)

"Humans can bring out treasures from the depths of the earth" (28:1-11)

There are many wonderful things that human beings can do. The poet talks about mining, giving examples of human ingenuity in bringing metals and precious stones from the depths of the earth. Humans have probed beneath the surface where all is dark (v. 3) and far from any human habitation (v. 4). They have seen things that even the birds have not seen (v. 7) and have walked where even the mightiest beasts have never been (v. 8). The miners have virtually turned mountains inside out, exposing to light those things that have always been hidden (vv. 9 and 11). This is all quite wonderful. Humans have the ability to shed light on what had been concealed, to uncover what had been shrouded in mystery.

One can imagine that if a modern poet were to make a similar point, he or she might well use our exploration in space as an example of the technological prowess of the human race.

"But they cannot find or buy wisdom" (28:12-22)

In spite of all these accomplishments, wisdom remains elusive, beyond the reach of any living human being (vv. 12 and 13). Though we can know much and achieve much, there are always gaps and limits in our understanding. We cannot see the whole picture, we cannot see how all things connect, we do not know how today's events fit into God's future. The "Deep" and the "Sea" in v. 14 probably refer to supernatural beings (cf. 7:12) who, though mightier than humans in power and insight, still do not have true wisdom.

Wisdom cannot be bought with gold or silver or precious stones (vv. 15-19). No amount of precious metal or jewels brought forth from the ground can be compared to the value of wisdom. Even if humans could amass huge fortunes, they would be useless in the acquisition of wisdom.

Verse 20 repeats the question of v. 12. Where can one go to find wisdom? It is hid from all living creatures, even from the high-flying birds who can look down on the earth from their lofty perspective and see more than creatures who are unable to fly. Even Death and Abaddon (another name for Sheol, the place of the dead; see 26:6) only know rumors about wisdom. They do not possess wisdom themselves, but only pass on what they have heard elsewhere.

In the first two sections of this chapter, then, we have been told that humans have accomplished many wonderful things but they still have not found (and are incapable of finding) wisdom.

"Only God knows where to find it" (28:23-28)

God, and only God, knows where wisdom is to be found (v. 23). God sees everything that happens from one end of the world to the other (v. 24). God has known wisdom since the time of creation. When God was setting up the wind and measuring out the bodies of water (v. 25) and organizing the rain and the thunderstorms (v. 26), then God saw wisdom. We are not completely sure what is meant here. It is almost as if Wisdom is a person, as if she existed along with God at the beginning of time. There are biblical passages that talk about wisdom that way. For example, in Prov. 8:22-31 Wisdom speaks and declares that she was created first by God, at the beginning of God's creative activity, and then worked with God to complete the creation. This view of Wisdom has often been seen as important for the "Word" theology of John 1. "In the beginning was the Word, and the Word was with God, and the Word was God" (John 1:1).

The writer of Job 28 may or may not have in mind the image of Wisdom as a person (as Proverbs 8). The point, however, is clearly that God has a relationship with Wisdom which is impossible for any other creature—human, demonic, or otherwise. There are things that only God knows, and no amount of human effort can bridge that gap.

What is possible for humans is to fear God and be obedient to God, i.e., depart from evil (v. 28). Though humans cannot come to complete knowledge on their own, God has not left them in the dark. God lets them know what they need to know. So, if humans approach God with fear (reverence, awe, a sense of worship), God will tell them how to live and will take care of the uncertainties of life which will always remain. If one trusts God and is obedient, one need not know the answer to every question. The elusiveness of wisdom is no tragedy.

Some scholars do not think that v. 28 is an original part of the rest of the chapter. They argue that it introduces a different way of talking about wisdom and they point out that the word for "Lord" (*'adonāy*) is used only here in the book of Job. Neither of these arguments seems compelling. The bigger question is whether Chap. 28 belongs to the original author. Verse 28 is not necessarily distinct from the rest of this chapter.

B. JOB'S FINAL SOLILOQUY (CHAPTERS 29–31)

The debates are over. The three friends are silent. Job brings this long section of the book to a close with some revealing and poignant words about his past, his present, and his continuing bewilderment about why he should be suffering.

The Way It Was (Chapter 29)

"In the old days, all was right with God and my neighbor" (29:1-10)

In Chap. 29, Job allows himself to think about how pleasant life used to be. In vv. 2-6, Job talks about the kind of relationship that he used to have with God. He longs for the days when God watched over him (v. 2), lightened his darkness (v. 3), and was still his friend (vv. 4-5). Then his children were with him (v. 5) and everything turned out right for him (v. 6). Sadly, Job is saying that none of this is his anymore. God is no longer a friend who is present with him. What a sad thing for a person of faith to say: "God is no longer with me to give support and lighten the way through the dark valleys." Job knows that he has lost something precious. The contrast between what used to be and what is now is terrible.

The loss of his close relationship with God is perhaps the most painful result of Job's suffering. But he has also lost the respect of his fellow human beings. Taken together, this puts Job in total isolation, with no one to care for and love him in his time of suffering and sorrow. In the old days, when

Job came into the city square, young and old alike gave him respect (vv. 7-8). Even the princes and nobles were quiet, waiting in expectation for a word of wisdom from the honored Job.

Those were the good days, Job's golden years, when all was right with God and humanity. Can such times ever be retrieved once they are lost? Will God return as before? Will human disgrace be replaced by acceptance and love?

"I was honored because of my good deeds" (29:11-17)

Job was well regarded by the people for good reasons. He was a model citizen, a marvelous example of one who carried out the ancient teachings of the Law and the Prophets that one should care for the poor, the widow, the orphan, the physically disabled, the stranger. (In 22:5-9, Eliphaz accused Job of not doing this. If we assume that Eliphaz was lying, can we assume that Job was as good as he says he was?) Job paints a picture of himself as a true and obedient follower of God's Law. He has always done what is proper. Perhaps we detect a note of exaggeration, an overstatement of the case, but we must remember that from the very first chapter Job has been presented as a good and upright man. There is no reason to doubt the basic truth of what Job says here. What is more worrisome is the connection he makes between his sterling ethical record and his expectation for a trouble-free life. He still expects the doctrine of retribution to work.

"I expected a good and long life" (29:18-20)

Job thought that the good life that he described in 29:1-10 would go on and on. Why shouldn't it? Job had been careful to do what a good religious person is supposed to do. Surely God would reward him for his good deeds. He could expect to die after a peaceful old age, in his own place, with his children around him, full of vigor to the end. But it did not turn out that way. And Job, as many other religious people, felt betrayed, because he had done his part but God had not upheld God's end of the bargain. If one expects to be rewarded for pious deeds, the disillusionment can be overwhelming when the anticipated rewards are not forthcoming.

"I had respect" (29:21-25)

These verses return again to the theme of respect for Job and his words. In fact, this passage flows so naturally from what was said in vv. 7-10 that some scholars have suggested that it is out of place in our Bibles and should be placed after v. 10 (for example, see the JB).

If what Job says is true, his suffering cost him dearly in terms of human relationships. He had been one whose counsel was sought by all, whose every word was anticipated with great expectations (vv. 21-23). His smile could inspire courage and he was known as one who brings comfort. Here is the picture of a benevolent father, almost kingly in his dignity, yet kind and caring for the needs of others. This is how Job imagined himself in the good old days. But now respect was gone. He was a beaten and lonely man, accused by his friends as the cause of his own trouble, uncertain about God and God's ways with the world, pessimistic and doubtful about the future. What a contrast to the man who gave comforting words of advice to others! No one would come to him with their troubles anymore.

"But Now Things Are Terrible" (Chapter 30)

Chapter 29 had been a nostalgia trip, an excursion into the past, hauling into the memory the pleasantries about how life used to be before the roof caved in. Chapter 29 was about the past, but was already intimating the present because the glorious past no longer existed. Now, in Chap. 30, Job goes into detail in his description of what the present is like.

"Even the rabble now mock me" (30:1-15)

Job speaks of the deep humiliation of being mocked by people who are much inferior to him. They are younger than he (v. 1). Their fathers were so disreputable that Job would not even have trusted them to guard the sheep with the dogs (and to be unworthy even to mingle with the dogs was a powerful insult indeed!) (v. 1). These people are some kind of outcasts (v. 8) who live on the outskirts of the community in caves and gullies (v. 6), eking out an existence by scavenging what they can from the inhospitable ground (vv. 3-4). Even such miserable people as these have now turned on Job. They have taken delight in his fall from prestige. They make fun of him (v. 9), imagine they are better than he (v. 10 "they keep aloof from me"), spit on him (v. 10b), and generally make his life miserable in any way that they can (vv. 12-14).

This is an interesting passage. One can only imagine who these "hoboes" are. As Job describes his own personal degradation, it is particularly painful to him that he should be ridiculed by the likes of these people. It is bad enough if those in your own social class turn against you, but these miserable creatures are not even worthy to guard Job's sheep. Some scholars have worried that Job sounds overly cruel toward these people, too self-conscious of his own status, perhaps revealing a kind of pompous patronizing in his attitude toward the poor and needy, a "Lady Bountiful" type of philanthropy which is willing to help the poor as long as they stay in their place. Maybe some of those same poor souls who benefited from Job's deeds of mercy were now the ones mocking the fall of the great benefactor.

"God has turned cruel to me" (30:16-23)

The rest of this chapter sounds much like a typical lament and is not very different from words of Job that we have encountered earlier in the book. He talks about constant pain that does not let up during day or night (vv. 16-17). God is named as the one who has caused all of Job's trouble (vv. 19-23). That is the logical conclusion to which Job has been driven by his belief in God's power and his insistence on his own innocence. As in other laments, Job reports that he has cried to God for help but has received no answer (v. 20). God has become cruel to Job (v. 21). The days when God was a caring friend (29:2-5) are long gone. God's cruelty is shown both in the misery which he has brought to Job but also in God's refusal to answer when Job cries for help. The sufferer receives too much of God (everything bad that happens is somehow God's doing) *and* too little of God (because God does not answer the sufferer's prayer). If only God would either go away and leave Job alone *or* would speak to Job to assure him. At this point, all that Job can see ahead is death. God is bringing him to his death, the end that comes to all living creatures (v. 23).

"I looked for good, but evil came" (30:24-31)

As he continues his lament, Job again speaks of his disappointment in receiving troubles in spite of his good works (as in 29:18-20). He had wept with people who were having a hard time and had grieved for the poor (v. 25). As one reared with a belief in divine retribution, he expected good to come, but instead came evil and darkness rather than light (v. 26).

Job concludes this lament by talking about his blackened skin (vv. 28, 30), his kinship with jackals and ostriches, and how mourning and weeping have replaced the joyful sounds of lyre and pipe that were appropriate earlier in his life (v. 31). His darkened skin probably is a description of his disease. His identification with jackals and ostriches may be because his cry of lament is similar to their melancholy cry or because their loneliness out in the desert is like his separation from God and other human beings.

"Does Not Calamity Befall the Unrighteous?" (Chapter 31)

"If retribution works, then I should be all right" (31:1-34, 38-40)

Here at the end of his speeches, Job is still struggling with the doctrine of retribution. He has never really rejected it. He still expects that it should work, that the righteous should be rewarded and the wicked punished (31:3-4). His complaint is that God has not acted with justice according to the rules that Job had learned. He, the good man, is suffering, while examples of prosperous wicked people abound. Job cannot let go of the doctrine of retribution. It is too important for his ideas of justice and how God works in the world. In this chapter he speaks out of both bewilderment and protest. If he had been a bad person and had committed all sorts of sins (many of which he lists in this chapter), he would have expected to be punished. But since he did not do any of these things, his suffering (which seems like punishment) makes no sense. So Job still wonders what went wrong, indirectly protesting what has happened to him. (In earlier chapters, his complaints about God's justice had been much more direct.)

Most of Chap. 31 is a series of "if" clauses. Job lists many sins that are considered by his religious tradition to be worthy of punishment. In each case, he proposes that if he had, in fact, committed such a sin, he would expect unpleasant consequences. The implication is that he has not done any of these things and therefore should not be experiencing all these calamities.

He lists a wide variety of possible infractions of the Law. He is concerned not only with outward behavior but also with inner motivation. Some scholars have compared this passage from Job positively with the Sermon on the Mount, where Jesus talks of inner emotions (such as lust and hate) which are to be condemned as much as the actual misdeed. Among those sins which Job lists are deceit (vv. 5-6), adultery (vv. 9-12), failure to assist the weak and helpless (servants, the poor, widows, and orphans, vv. 13-23), idolatry (vv. 24-28), rejoicing at the misfortune of one's enemy (vv. 29-30), and acquiring another's land wrongfully (vv. 38-40). In effect, Job says a curse upon himself. If he has been guilty of any of these sins, then he should be punished. Job must be a very self-confident person to put his body on the line in this way. He is certain that he has done no wrong. Is any human being that good—even Job? To those of us who have been taught that we are all sinners and continually deceive ourselves about how good we are, Job's statements sound a bit overstated. Speaking relatively, Job may still be the best example available of a pious and faithful servant of God. At least compared to others, Job may be less deserving of his troubles than they. But we may wonder if Job has not gone too far in protesting his innocence.

"If only I knew what I have done" (31:35-37)

These three verses seem to be out of place. One would expect them at the end of the chapter, after all the curses have ended. Instead, vv. 38-40 return to the theme of sins for which Job claims not to be guilty. There seems to be no good explanation for this order.

Job, speaking out of his own integrity, cannot see why he deserves all that has happened to him. When his counselors urged him to confess his guilt, he honestly could not do it because he did not know what he had done that was wrong. In this chapter he is still protesting that he has not committed any sin grave enough to have brought on all his troubles. But, if God will speak to him and lay out the charges against him, then he will listen and accept and even proudly wear the indictment like an article of clothing so that all can see. Though Job claims to be innocent, he is at least open to the possibility that God can tell him something that his friends have not been able to tell him, that he may have sinned in some way that he has not yet understood. As long as God remains silent, there is no way that Job can discover what has gone wrong and what he can do to remedy it.

So Job demands an audience with God. He will tell God all that he has done. He is not ashamed of his record. He has not been beaten down by all that has happened. He still has his integrity. He will approach God like a prince. He expects to get a fair hearing. Job thinks he can make a good case for his innocence, but if God has a case against him, Job will listen.

So the words of Job are ended (v. 40b). The discussions between Job and his friends began with a lament by Job (Chap. 3) and they end with a soliloquy by Job. We sense that the next move is up to God. Either God will come to meet Job or not. Either God will explain to Job why he has been suffering or not. Job has nothing more to say. Eliphaz, Bildad, and Zophar—thankfully—have already stepped aside. Maybe God will now finally speak.

C. SOME THEOLOGICAL AND PASTORAL CONSIDERATIONS

1. When does one stop asking questions?

For many long pages, Job and his three friends wrestled with the "Why?" questions. Why is Job suffering? Why does God allow good people to be hurt? Why is there so much injustice in a world in which God rules? Why do the wicked prosper? And so on. Is there a time, finally, when one can loosen up on the compulsion to find answers? Chapter 28 suggests that human wisdom is limited, that some mystery will always remain, that only God knows all the answers. Our problem is to make distinctions between what is knowable for a human and what isn't. In Chaps. 29 and 31 Job seems not yet able to make those distinctions. He still demands answers from God. He is not yet satisfied that his questions have been seriously considered. The words of Chap. 28 are for us, the readers. Job cannot yet hear them. Something more must happen before he is ready to relinquish his search. Perhaps at a later time he can accept the mystery and trust God anyway. But he is not yet ready.

Some people take longer than others before they can back away from their pursuit of the hard questions. Though it is a truism that humans cannot know everything, such a word to a sufferer may not be heard as good news. We will need to mention this point again after we look at God's speeches (Chaps. 38–41) and try to understand why Job apparently accepts then what he is not able to accept at this point.

2. Chapter 28 does not propose a blind antiintellectualism.

To be sure, the message is that wisdom is elusive and only God knows where wisdom is to be found. But the first part of the chapter gives praise to the accomplishments of humans, the ability to dig deep into unknown, dark, faraway places and uncover what had formerly been unknown. There are many things that humans can do. Too often the church has so emphasized the limits of human wisdom that it has virtually negated human intelligence and its possibilities of discovery. The church has often protected itself and its traditional ways from inquiring minds by pleading that humans can never know God's mysteries. We have two dangers, then, with which to contend. On the one hand, we are warned of human pride which seeks to know and control as only God can. On the other, we have a belittling of human capacity which begs off our responsibility to be stewards of creation, appointed by God to have dominion over the earth.

3. What is the value of nostalgia?

In Chap. 29, Job talks in glowing terms about how wonderful his world used to be. Many of us can relate well to what he is saying. As people get older, as their various losses accumulate, they look back on their days of strength and happiness. Often, the past begins to look better and better as we increase our distance from it. Sometimes a whole society seems to go through a time of nostalgia, when the past seems much more appealing than the present. Some have even made the 1930s (days of depression) and the 1940s (war and Hitler and death camps and atomic bombs) into the "good old days."

No doubt Job's early life was better than his later suffering. He needs to be free to voice his pain about all that he has lost, to be allowed to grieve over what can never be replaced. Remembering the past helps us to come to terms with it. Talking about it helps us to let go of it so that we can find new meaning in the present and hope for the future. But if remembering becomes nostalgia, overly sentimental and yearning for a return to a past that is no longer recoverable, then it has moved from a healthy remembrance to an unhealthy attachment to the past.

4. Job is still trapped in the doctrine of retribution.

At the very end of his speeches, Job still talks in terms of proper retribution, what is just and what isn't, what he deserves and what is unfair. He still contemplates a meeting with God which will be like a court scene, in which evidence is presented and a judgment is made. God, the judge, will either accept Job on the basis of his ethical record and withdraw the punishment or God will make known some secret accusation which is not yet known to Job. If the latter is the outcome, Job will take it "like a man" and be proud to let his indictment from God be seen by all.

As we shall see, God will not respond to Job according to Job's expectations. Such courtroom analogies, though often used by religious folk, are not the only, and may not be the best, images for describing the relationship between God and human beings. Our acceptance by God is not based on a judicial appraisal of our good works.

5. Job shows an unpleasant side in his concluding soliloquy.

During the dialogs with Job, his friends became increasingly convinced that Job was not such a perfect person after all. The way that he talked about himself, other people, and God gave hints of pride, defensiveness, hostility, and other all-too-human attributes. Eliphaz tells Job that Job's own mouth condemns him and his own lips testify against him (15:6).

As we read Job's words in Chaps. 29–31, we, too, see some aspects of Job's character that we do not like. In 30:1-15, he seems particularly elitist and prejudicial in his attitude toward the disreputable, useless, band of no-bodies who now dare to mock him. Chapter 29 (and other passages) seems to show a condescending attitude toward the poor and needy whom he stoops to help out of his great compassion. As mentioned earlier, he seems a bit prideful in his disclaimer about never committing any of the sins listed in Chap. 31. Some have also talked about his lack of humility in 31:37 where he talks as if he, a mere mortal, will be able to come before God like a prince.

All of this raises questions against the backdrop of the doctrine of retribution. Though we were told in Chaps. 1 and 2 that Job was innocent and good and upright, we may be tempted to see Job as a sinner after all, to fall back on the doctrine of retribution, to absolve God from any part in Job's miseries, and to think that we really understand why Job suffered. We ought not judge Job in this way. He remains an innocent sufferer. The book of Job intends to show that the doctrine of retribution does not always work in this life. There are questions that must remain unanswered (Chaps. 28; 38–41), and to presume that we have found the answer in Job's guilt is to be untrue to the purpose of the book of Job.

6

The Speeches of Elihu
(Job 32–37)

Chapters 32–37 seem to be a break in the continuity. The end of Chap. 31 invites a response from God. The words of Job and his three friends are ended and, if God is ever going to speak, now is the time. There is a natural flow from Chap. 31 to Chap. 38. If Chaps. 32–37 were missing, you would not even notice.

A majority of Job scholars thinks that Chaps. 32–37 were added to the book of Job later. They were not written by the great author of Chaps. 3–31 and Chaps. 38–41. There are a number of compelling reasons for this consensus. As mentioned above, Elihu's speeches in 32–37 break the flow of the book. Elihu is not mentioned before Chap. 32 and is not named in 42:7-9, where the other three counselors are held accountable for their dealings with Job. The style and the language in these chapters are different. In previous chapters, the method of presentation was to let each counselor speak in turn and then let Job reply. In these six chapters, only Elihu speaks. It is strictly a monolog. This means that we have no way of knowing whether Job accepts any of Elihu's words or, more likely, if he continues to contend with both the content and pastoral style of his counselors. There are many indications of the influence of Aramaic on the text of Job, but examples of this are more prominent in the Elihu speeches. Further, Elihu indicates that he knows what Job had said earlier in the book and sometimes quotes Job's words back to him. It is conceivable that the original author might use this device, but it looks as though a later hand is making further commentary on the prior discussion. That is to say, someone is trying to improve on a book of Job which already exists.

Whether or not the Elihu speeches are written by the author of most of the rest of the book, the question remains whether these speeches have much value. Opinions differ with regard to this question, though the majority would probably dismiss Elihu as rather irrelevant, neither adding to nor detracting from the total message of the book. One could ask the question of its value from two directions. First, does it add anything to the content of the argument, the questions about why Job or anyone else should suffer? Second, is it important to the flow of the book? We have already shared the conclusion of the majority that it is not and its absence would not be noticed. There are, however, some who feel that the Elihu speeches play an important part in the process of moving Job out of his rut as a complainer to a position where he can accept his situation. According to this line of thought, the Elihu speeches prepare Job, perhaps psychologically or theologically, for the speeches of God. Some argue that Elihu's intervention makes it possible for Job to hear when God speaks in Chap. 38.[27]

These chapters can be divided into four speeches, if we assume that we are beginning a new speech each time the text tells us that Elihu speaks. At any rate, no matter how we count the speeches, Elihu is the only one who talks. We shall look at each of the four speeches in some detail.

Elihu's First Speech (Chapters 32–33)

Prose introduction (32:1-5)

The Elihu section begins with a short introduction written in prose. It provides a transition to tell us who Elihu is and why he began to speak. We are told that the three previous counselors ceased speaking to Job because of his self-righteousness (v. 1). Certainly Job had concluded with a stirring defense of his integrity (Chaps. 29–31). He did protest that he was a good person and did not deserve his terrible fate. But is that self-righteousness, as the writer of this section states? Is that what ended the conversation with Eliphaz and the others? The dialogs had to end sometime. For those of us who had labored through all the arguments of the second and third cycle, it was a relief that the counselors finally chose silence. The author of the dialog apparently intended to end the debates with Job's conclusion and get on to the speeches of God.

Elihu is introduced as an angry man (vv. 2, 3, 5). He is angry with Job
because he justified himself rather than God (v. 3). He was angry at Job's
three friends because they could find no way to answer Job's charges against
God (vv. 3, 4).

It is true that Job blamed God rather than himself for his trouble. He
refused to think worse of himself in order to make God look good. Both Job
and his friends were stuck in a dilemma that is common for sufferers. They
had to blame someone. And the choices were limited to God and Job (none
of the human beings in the story ever suggests Satan as a possible source of
Job's trouble). With only two options, Job does indeed blame God rather than
himself. And Job's friends, as theologians are usually inclined to do, see as
their task to defend God against Job's attacks. Their conclusion, then, is that
God could not possibly be at fault, and Job must be the culprit.

Elihu's anger at the failure of the three counselors to find an answer to
Job implies that there must be an answer. It suggests the possibility that if
we just stay with this argument a bit longer, we can come up with some
intellectual formulation which will successfully explain why Job has suffered
and will make clear that God has not been unjust in any of this. It may be
that the text at the end of v. 3 originally said that Job's friends had condemned
God (though perhaps indirectly), because of their inability to refute Job's
statements. To stop too soon in the discussion could be seen as conceding the
argument to Job and accepting Job's criticisms of God.[28] One can imagine
that Elihu (that is, the later author who inserted this material) might have
thought this and therefore felt compelled to add to the book. Another way to
understand v. 3 is to follow the RSV and read "although they had declared
Job to be in the wrong." They certainly had done that.[29]

Verse 4 gives a reason why, in spite of his anger, Elihu had waited so
long to speak. The others were all older than he so, out of deference to their
age, he had waited till they were finished before he began. This is a useful
device for introducing a new character into the conversation. If the book of
Job was already in existence, perhaps even widely known, at the time of the
writing of the speeches of Elihu, this literary technique would be a way of
justifying the validity of a new statement to correct and amplify what was
already written. The old-timers need not have the last word. There is something new that can be said which might even improve on what was handed
down to us by a previous generation.

"God's spirit, not one's age, gives wisdom" (32:6-10)

After the prose introduction, Elihu begins to speak. He puts into words
the same argument that was already mentioned in v. 4 of the introduction.

Elihu had been holding back his opinion because of respect for those who were older. Finally, he comes to the conclusion that it is not merely age that brings wisdom (v. 9). Much more important than age is whether or not one has God's spirit (v. 8). Elihu assumes that he has the spirit and is entitled to speak.

"I can wait no longer; I must speak" (32:11-22)

Elihu, in a rather wordy, almost pretentious style, continues to elaborate on what had already been stated briefly in the prose introduction. Elihu had waited for some refutation of Job (vv. 11-12), but it did not come. The wisdom of the three has not been demonstrated (v. 13). Elihu will pick up the discussion and proceed in a different way from them (v. 14). He is no longer willing to wait for them to think of something more to say. It has become clear that they have exhausted their wisdom on this subject. Elihu will now give his answer (vv. 15-17). Elihu is so full of words needing to be expressed that he is like a new wineskin that is ready to burst (vv. 18-19). He must speak in order to find relief (v. 20).

Elihu claims that in his remarks he will not show partiality or flattery toward any human being (v. 21). He says that he is incapable of flattery and that God would punish him anyway if he engaged in such an approach to persons. Elihu may be making reference here to Job's complaint in Chap. 13 that his counselors were all on God's side instead of on his. They automatically assumed that in any argument about God's justice the human being (Job) must be wrong, because God could not possibly be in the wrong. Job accused them of speaking falsely for God (13:7) and showing partiality toward God (13:8). Elihu says he will not be partial. Some scholars who appreciate Elihu for his straight and blunt approach to Job, point to this verse as evidence that Elihu will be an improvement over the other counselors, who certainly did prejudice the case against Job. The problem with that understanding of Elihu is that he does not live up to his own statement. He is not at all impartial. Already in this chapter we have been told that Elihu was angry because Job justified himself rather than God (32:2) and because the counselors had not been able to counter Job's statement (that is, to demonstrate adequately that God really is just). Elihu may be impartial in disputes between human beings (32:21), but in a dispute between a human being and God there is no doubt whatsoever that Elihu is on God's side. Before we finish the Elihu speeches we will again see that Job is condemned and God is defended.

"Listen to my words" (33:1-7)

It takes a long time for Elihu to get started. He is still talking about himself and his sincerity and integrity (v. 3). He had earlier mentioned that it is God's spirit and not merely age that imparts wisdom (32:8). He claims that God's spirit made him and resides in him (v. 4). Whether or not that makes him any different from anyone else is not clear. He does seem to be claiming an authority for his message. Verse 2 is an odd way to begin speaking. If one of your friends began a conversation with you with such self-conscious, affected, bloated words, you might wonder, "Just who does he think he is anyway?"

Verses 5-7 are important words for those who like Elihu. He invites Job to an open conversation about these significant matters. Elihu says, "Answer me, if you can" (v. 5a). The writer of the Elihu speeches, however, does not allow Job to answer. Does that imply that Elihu has made his case so well that Job is incapable of challenging his wisdom? It is hard to believe that the Job who had so thoroughly demolished the arguments of the other three counselors (many of them similar to those of Elihu) would be silent in response to Elihu's invitation to debate. In vv. 6-7, we have Elihu at his best. He is a human being like Job. They are equals as they participate in the struggle to make sense out of life's misfortunes. Elihu implies that he does not know any more than Job, that they are in this mess together, that Job need not regard Elihu as an authority who is trying to impose his own rationalizations about suffering on him. If Elihu really means this, if he really has that kind of humility before Job and the mysteries of life, then he clearly is an improvement over the other three counselors, and one who could possibly teach us something positive about pastoral care. Unfortunately, it seems that Elihu does not perform as he promises. He will condemn Job and justify God and claim superiority for his words over everything that Job has said earlier in the book. So much for the "we're in this together" approach.

"Job, you are wrong to claim innocence" (33:8-12)

With all the preliminaries out of the way, Elihu now gets down to the basic discussion. Elihu knows what Job has been saying earlier in the book. According to Elihu, Job has claimed that he is without iniquity (v. 9) and God has acted against him as an enemy, seeking occasions to hurt Job without any good reason (vv. 10-11). In short, Job has said that he does not deserve his suffering and the fault lies with God.

Elihu has probably heard Job correctly. Time after time, Job has said words to this effect. Like a good pastoral counselor, Elihu has summed up for Job what he has been saying. The TEV even translates Elihu's words into the jargon of modern pastoral counseling, "Now this is what I heard you say" (v. 8). But then come the blunt, confrontational words of judgment by Elihu. "Job, you are wrong. God can't be wrong. Humans can't be pure and innocent. God is greater than man" (v. 12b). Theological presuppositions have already determined who is right and who is wrong in this debate. So much for Elihu's impartiality. Job is wrong. God is right.

"God *does* speak to us" (33:13-30)

Job, like many lamenters, longed for a word from God. The silence of God is very difficult for a sufferer. One cries for relief, some explanation, at least an indication that the prayer has even been heard. When one most needs the comforting assurance of God's presence is often the time when God seems most remote. Elihu, again responding to what he has heard from Job, tries to deal rationally with Job's complaint by pointing out that God in fact does speak to us, in several different ways, even though we humans are not able to perceive it (v. 14). This is an important section for the content of Elihu's message.

God speaks to human beings in dreams, in visions of the night (one is reminded of Eliphaz in 4:12-21). Even terrifying dreams may be a message from God. Their purpose is to warn human beings to change their ways and avert disaster (vv. 16-18). God also speaks through the suffering itself. God chastens people by their pain and illness (v. 19). Unfortunately, we are not always able to interpret the illness correctly. In vv. 19-28, Elihu talks about one who becomes so ill that he is very close to death (v. 22). At that point, just as all seems lost, God sends an angel or mediator, one who will speak on behalf of the ill person before God (vv. 24-26). Then the man turns to God and is accepted (v. 26). Out of gratitude, the man who has been saved will sing the praises of God before others, telling them that even though he has been a sinner who deserved punishment, God in his mercy had saved him from death (vv. 26-28).

Elihu makes several key points here: *(a)* You are wrong to say that God does not answer your prayer. Though you may not know it, God speaks to you in many ways—through dreams, through your experiences (even un-pleasant ones such as illness), and by sending an angel (or messenger or mediator) to help interpret your experience and speak on your behalf. *(b)* Suffering is often for the purpose of chastening, of education, in order to teach a person to correct his or her behavior before it leads to more serious consequences. *(c)* Suffering is never something that God brings arbitrarily, but only for good reasons. *(d)* Out of his mercy, God not only sends a mediator but also indicates that God will listen to the one who pleads on our behalf (see 16:19-21; 19:25-27; also 9:33). In short, God wants to deliver us and is looking for an excuse. It is a little uncertain what ransom is offered (in v. 24b) in order to buy one's redemption from the Pit. Such thoughts as these remind us of ways in which Christians have tried to explain the work of Jesus Christ in delivering us from the consequences of our sins. *(e)* Humans are sinners who bring suffering on themselves. When the moment of enlightenment comes (v. 27), the one who has been delivered confesses that he did indeed deserve the punishment of death, but God had delivered him and given him further life (v. 28). Elihu supports the doctrine of retribution (humans deserve what happens to them) but he also extends the idea to say that suffering may have a positive educative value in helping us make corrections before it is too late. At any rate, Job is a sinner who thus far has not heeded the message that God is sending.

In several ways Elihu reminds us of Eliphaz, who spoke of visions in the night, who supported the doctrine of retribution (e.g., 4:7-9), and who referred to suffering as the chastening of the Almighty (5:17).

"Listen to me, Job" (33:31-33)

Again, Elihu tells Job to listen to him. If Job has something to say, he is invited to speak up. As mentioned, however, Job will remain silent, thus seeming to condone the words spoken by Elihu. Elihu says he would be glad to justify Job, that is, to find him innocent (v. 32). But Job's silence apparently indicates that such an outcome is impossible. Elihu continues to sound rather arrogant—"Be silent, and I will teach you wisdom" (v. 33).

Elihu's Second Speech (Chapter 34)

"Job is an enemy of true religion" (34:1-9)

In vv. 1-4, Elihu addresses some wise men and invites them to look at the facts and make a judgment about Job. Perhaps he is talking to others like himself who had been standing by listening to the earlier discussion with Eliphaz and the others. Perhaps it is merely a rhetorical device to draw the reader into the discussion. He is probably not talking to Eliphaz, Bildad, and Zophar, after the way he has dismissed them for their lack of wisdom (as in 32:11-16).

Elihu reminds one of a politician who picks over his opponent's speeches, removes quotes from context, and then proceeds to assume all sorts of negative characteristics about his rival on the basis of those quotes. Elihu has looked at Job's words and, by and large, has heard them correctly. But he has removed them from the context of a sufferer who is desperately trying to maintain his integrity and make sense of his situation. Like Eliphaz and the others before him, Elihu takes Job's questioning words, spoken out of great pain and confusion, and sees them as the words of a scoffer, an enemy of religion, one who would lead astray the ordinary pious person by raising doubts about the value of true belief in God (v. 9).

In vv. 5-8, Elihu, obviously not speaking impartially as he has promised, says that Job, far from being innocent and without transgression as he claims, is actually a scoffer who keeps company with evildoers. Job's great sin, it seems, is that he has said, "It profits a man nothing that he should take delight in the Lord" (v. 9). Certainly Job has said things like this. From his own experience and from his observations of others, Job has come to the conclusion that the doctrine of retribution does not work, and innocent people are just as likely to meet disaster as the wicked (e.g., 9:22). In 21:14-15, Job quotes the wicked people who scoff at God, who have not seen God's justice at work, and therefore think they are immune from God's judgment. They have decided that there is no profit for them in serving God and therefore they do not. Job himself does not agree with the way the wicked have used this conclusion to justify their evil ways. But Eliphaz (in 22:17) and now Elihu accuse Job of preaching that there is no reward in serving God.

Why do human beings serve God? Is Satan right after all when he suggests (1:9-11) that we serve God only for rewards that we will receive or punishment that we will avoid? Eliphaz and Elihu seem to agree with Satan. They say, "If you take away the incentive of rewards and punishment, human beings will not serve God." Since Job is raising questions about the working of this retributive system, he must be a dangerous, antireligious person. If people believe Job when he says God's system of justice doesn't work anymore, they will turn away from fear of God and proper ethical behavior and follow their own desires, to their ultimate harm.

"God is indeed just" (34:10-30)

In this section, Elihu gives a rather clear and straightforward defense of God's justice, impartiality, and power. Elihu continues to argue with Job, disputing Job's accusations about God's failure to act in a just manner. It would be unthinkable for God to do wrong (vv. 10 and 12). Verse 11 is about as direct a statement of the doctrine of retribution as one could find. God is just in giving people what they deserve. And God has the power to do it. The logic of this would lead one to say that everything that happens must be God's will and must be made to fit these axioms of God's justice and power. In such a system, there is no alternative but to fault Job for his problems. If God is both just and all-powerful it could not be otherwise.

God is all-powerful. No one else gave God charge over the earth (v. 13). God's spirit gives life, and if God should gather it back to himself all humans would perish (vv. 14-15). By definition, God is almighty and just. That is simply the way it is. Elihu seems almost too willing to assume that simply because one has the power to govern, it follows automatically that the ruler will govern with justice (v. 17). Elihu is not dealing with Job's experience nor his questions, which come from a real-life situation. Rather, Elihu starts with propositions about God which must be true no matter what our experience is. God acts impartially toward all, whether prince or commoner, rich or poor (v. 19). All are created by God and God has the power to do what God wants with them. God may even strike down the mighty who think they are invulnerable to danger from any human hand (v. 20).

In vv. 21-30, Elihu elaborates more fully on the themes of God's justice, power, and omniscience. God sees everything we do. There is no place where anyone can hide from God's eyes (vv. 21-22). Again, one is reminded of Eliphaz, who disputes the claim of the wicked that God cannot see them and judge them through the deep darkness and thick clouds that "enwrap him" (22:13-14). God does not have to answer to anyone about the way God is executing justice. God does what God wants in his own time and without investigation (vv. 24-25). God can do this because God knows what people have been doing and the sins which they have committed (vv. 25-28). God does not act without good reason. God is always just. We cannot condemn God because we do not understand what God is doing or because we think God is quiet and doing nothing to judge the wicked (v. 29).

In short, Elihu defends God as just, impartial, all-knowing, and all-powerful. Any criticism of God is inappropriate for human beings. Everything God does is just, whether or not we can understand it.

"Job is sinful and rebellious" (34:31-37)

The Hebrew of vv. 31-33 is very difficult to understand. If one compares several of the recent translations, it is obvious that there is no clear consensus about what is being said.

The meaning of vv. 34-37, however, is much less difficult. Elihu speaks of wise men who will surely agree with him about his judgment on Job. Perhaps, Elihu is referring to the wise men whom he had addressed at the beginning of this chapter (v. 2). If they consider the data he has presented they will confirm Elihu's conclusion that Job does not know what he is talking about (v. 35) and, further, he actually sounds like a wicked man (v. 36). Besides the sins which first brought on his suffering, he adds the sin of rebellion by speaking against God and God's justice (v. 37). Job appears on the surface to be a good person. But since God acts only in just ways, there must be a reason for Job's suffering. Therefore, Job is a sinner, and his continual denial of his guilt and heaping of abuse on God only demonstrate more and more obviously what kind of person Job really is. Once more we are reminded of Eliphaz in 15:6, "Your own mouth condemns you, and not I; your own lips testify against you."

Elihu had boasted that he had something new to say. He would not let the matter lie, leaving the possibility that if Job had not been properly answered, then God might be in the wrong. Elihu says to the other three counselors, "I will not answer him with your speeches." Again, Elihu is unable to live up to his expectations. His words are much like what we have heard before, especially from the mouth of Eliphaz.

Elihu's Third Speech (Chapter 35)

"Your sin or righteousness does not affect God" (35:1-8)

Elihu begins by briefly referring to Job's question whether anyone is actually better off by serving God in obedience (vv. 2-3). As he looked at his own life, Job had good cause to wonder about such things. Then Elihu takes a slight turn and deals with the question of whether or not our transgressions or righteousness have any effect upon God (vv. 5-7). Can a human affect God? Isn't that giving too much power to human beings? God doesn't need humans. They can do nothing for God either positively or negatively. Whether Job is wicked or righteous obviously will have an effect on other human beings who will be either hurt or helped by his behavior (v. 8), but God is above all that.

This passage reminds us of an earlier discussion that was carried on between Job and his counselors (especially Eliphaz). Job had early complained that God pays too much attention to human sins, as if humans could be a threat to God (see 7:12-20). In 22:1-4, Eliphaz answers Job's complaint by protesting that God does not gain anything by our righteousness. The workings of the doctrine of retribution are almost automatic, for the benefit of humans, for the sake of order and justice in the world. But God doesn't care. Elihu seems to be repeating the same line of reasoning, making certain that we do not ascribe too much power for humans to influence God.

We discussed this theological point as we looked at 22:1-4. The view of Eliphaz and Elihu is certainly one-sided. The Bible abounds with examples of how God has been moved, angered, delighted, and so on, by the activity of human beings. Elihu and Eliphaz remove God too far from involvement in our lives. A caring God cannot help but be affected by what we do.

"God does not hear an empty cry" (35:9-16)

Elihu continues to argue against points that had been made earlier by Job. In this section he again tries to deal with the silence of God, the apparent lack of an answer when people cry out to God for help. Earlier, Elihu had said that God *does* answer, though humans often fail to hear, by dreams, our suffering, and the sending of angels (or messengers) (33:13-30). Now Elihu presents further thoughts on this subject. Maybe the problem of God's silence exists because people have merely cried out in a general way without properly directing that cry to God (vv. 9-11).

Many commentators have noted favorably the lovely phrase in v. 10 which describes God our Maker as the one "who gives songs in the night." Taken in isolation from the rest of Elihu's speech, that is a comforting image of a God who meets us in our darkness and gives us songs to sustain us till morning.

Another reason why God does not answer sufferers when they cry out is "because of the pride of evil men" (v. 12b). According to Elihu, God does not hear or regard an empty cry (v. 13). An "empty" cry may be a vain or meaningless cry, not really directed toward God at all but only a kind of "blowing in the wind," complaining in general about one's situation but not coming directly to the Lord. If this is what Elihu is saying, he makes a cruel judgment on all those desperate sufferers who have cried out to God for relief and have not been helped. Can all such cries be swept aside as "vain," uttered by prideful human beings who have not turned wholly to God? Must we pass some kind of "sincerity test" before God will listen to us? Job is further castigated because he not only fails to turn to God but even claims that he does not know where to find God (v. 14a; compare 23:1-9). Job's lament about God's absence is apparently used by Elihu as evidence that Job is one of those prideful persons who has not yet turned to God with humility. The chapter ends with more condemnation of Job for his empty talk and lack of knowledge (v. 16).

Elihu's Fourth Speech (Chapters 36–37)

"Again I say, God is just" (36:1-7)

Elihu has not finished yet. He has more to say "on God's behalf" (v. 2b). This clearly expresses what Elihu has been doing all along—speaking *on God's behalf* and, as is often the case for those who are zealous in defending God, against human beings (in general, and Job in particular). Elihu will reach into his own vast reservoir of knowledge to show how righteous God is (v. 3). With a remarkable lack of humility, Elihu claims that all his words are true and that he is an exceedingly wise man (v. 4). Once more Elihu puts forth his belief that God is all-powerful, impartial, all-knowing, and just. Maybe Elihu thinks that if he repeats these attributes often enough, Job will be convinced and believe them even though his own experience has called them into question. God does not keep the wicked alive (v. 6a, as against Job's speeches about the prosperity of the wicked) and God does not abandon the righteous (v. 7).

"God instructs us by our suffering" (36:8-15)

This is an important passage from Elihu, combining his belief in a doctrine of retribution with the idea that suffering can have a beneficial outcome if we heed the message that God intends. (See also similar ideas from Elihu in 33:13-30.) When people are caught in some sort of trouble (v. 8), God shows them what they have been doing wrong (v. 9). The suffering is a way of getting their attention. God uses it to "open their ears to instruction" (v. 10). If they hear and return to God, they will be blessed with prosperity (v. 11), but if they do not, they will perish (v. 12).

Suffering, then, performs two functions for Elihu. It is the result of human sin, the consequence of transgressions committed by human beings (v. 9). But God does not bring suffering on humans *only* as punishment. God's purpose is to teach us by our suffering so that we will turn back to him, put our lives in order, and live a good and long and happy life (v. 11). However, if we do not turn to God, if we do not heed the warning, the retribution doctrine again comes into play and we will perish, perhaps violently, certainly in ignorance (v. 12).

The godless hang on to their anger (Elihu may be thinking of Job here) and do not cry for help even when bound in affliction (v. 13). It is not completely clear what Elihu means here. It sounds similar to his words in 35:13 where he said, "Surely God does not hear an empty cry." The question seems to be whether one will continue to be angry with God for bringing on suffering, insisting that it is unjust, boasting of one's own innocence *or* whether one will be able to see his or her own responsibility in the onset of the trouble and will use the experience, as unpleasant as it is, to learn something of benefit. Those who cannot learn from the ordeal will die young and in shame (v. 14). But others will be delivered by their affliction, their eyes opened by their distress (v. 15).

"Take heed for yourself, Job" (36:16-21)

The text for these few verses is very difficult. A comparison of several translations shows a wide diversity as scholars have attempted to make sense out of the Hebrew. This much we can probably say: Elihu is now talking directly to Job, applying some of the general statements that he has just made. There is some kind of warning to Job, probably urging him to be one of those who learns from his suffering and does not continue in anger, scoffing, judging

God and God's work among humans. Finally, there seems to be a reference
to the purpose of his suffering (v. 21), including the hope that his suffering
will have the effect of preventing him from turning toward evil.

"God is exalted and to be praised" (36:22-26)

This is a transitional passage as we move from the main substance of
Elihu's message to the concluding hymn which extols God's wonderful works
in nature. Verses 22-23 sum up much of what has been said. God is the
supreme power. No one can compare with God as a teacher (even suffering
has its educative value). No one can tell God what to do or accuse God of
doing wrong. Then Elihu moves on to introduce a hymn in praise of God's
majesty. We extol God's work in the created order. The wonders of the universe
are there for us to see and be amazed at the Power that lies behind the created
world (v. 24). Yet, though we can see the results of God's labor, we cannot
see God. We can see only from a distance. We cannot understand all there
is to know about this complex and wondrous universe in which we live, nor
can we fully know the God who made it (vv. 25-26).

"We see God's majesty in nature" (36:27—37:13)

God is in charge of nature. God brings the weather. God brings the rain
(vv. 27-28), which is necessary for our food (v. 31). God's lightning and
thunder are reminders of the power of God's word and the swiftness with
which God brings judgment against iniquity (36:32—37:5). There are some
things which humans simply cannot understand—such as the formation of
clouds or the origin of the thunder (36:29). In 37:5, we are again reminded
that, even though we make a list of the wonders of creation, we cannot really
comprehend how or why God does all those things which we have on our
list. And so our observations of nature do two things for us: they give us
evidence of God's work *and* they remind us of how little we *really* know
about God's activity in the world.

In vv. 6-10, there is a further extolling of God's deeds, but now moving
into the cold season of the year. As God brings rain, so also God brings snow
(v. 6). Animals go into hibernation (v. 8), the cold winds come (v. 9), and
God's breath turns the water to ice (v. 10). The changes of seasons, the
designation of the place where lightning strikes, the formation and movement
of clouds, and the giving or withholding of rain are all God's doing (37:12
and elsewhere in this section). In all of this, God acts with purpose. There
is, for Elihu, no such thing as luck or chance, even in the formation of the
weather. God is behind it all, either for punishment or correction (if one is
at the wrong end of the thunderbolt or suffering from lack of rain or washed

away in a flood) or for love (God provides the cloud which produces the rain which makes possible the food which we need to survive) (v. 13). This is consistent with Elihu's view of a God who is all-powerful, who must be involved in all that happens, who is just and does not act contrary to justice. Since sometimes bad things happen to humans in the world of nature, such events are to be interpreted as judgment upon sin or as an effort by God to help us amend our ways and avoid further disasters.

"Job, do you know how God does this?" (37:14-24)

Elihu now speaks directly to Job, who is invited to consider all these wondrous works of God (v. 14). Elihu asks Job if he knows how God brings forth lightning (v. 15) or balances the clouds (v. 16). Can Job (like God) stretch out the sky (v. 18)? There may be a note of sarcasm here. Of course, Job has neither the knowledge nor the power. Elihu has already told us that there are many things we humans cannot understand (36:29 and 37:5). In vv. 19-20, the sarcasm becomes more obvious as Job is invited to teach us what to say to God (v. 19a). Job may want to make his case before God and may think he can come out ahead in such a confrontation, but Elihu thinks you are just asking for trouble if you get into that kind of contest with God (vv. 19b-20).

Some commentators suggest that vv. 21-22, returning to the theme of the wonders of nature (the brightness of the sky when the wind has blown the clouds away), is out of place here. The final two verses (vv. 23-24) again remind us that though we cannot know all about God, we can, nevertheless, be assured that God is powerful and just and will always act according to those attributes. It is no wonder that human beings stand in awe and reverence before God. Even the wisest of people are so inferior to God that they are beneath God's notice. Any pretentions toward wisdom on the part of humans is utter foolishness when compared with the wisdom of God.

There are obvious similarities between Elihu's concluding section and both Chap. 28 (the Wisdom poem) and Chaps. 38–41 (God's speeches). In all of these passages, God is presented as the only true source of wisdom, and the gap between human and divine understanding is highlighted. Elihu's questions to Job in 37:15-18 very much resemble God's address to Job in 38–41. Even the sarcastic edge to Elihu's speech is not unlike the tone of God's questioning of Job.

As mentioned before, some have doubted the authenticity of Chap. 28 because it "upstages" God. One could also ask that of Elihu's speech, but most people have already decided that the Elihu section is not original, anyway. The writer of Elihu's speeches completes the transition from Job's final words to God's opening words (though no transition was necessary) by closing with material very similar (and leading up) to what God is about to say. This has led some commentators to the conclusion that Elihu has helped in the process of moving Job forward to a stance of receptivity to God's message. After Chap. 28 Job was not ready to give up his own search for answers simply because God is wiser than human beings. He still may not be ready for that step after Elihu is finished (we don't know, of course, because the author does not have Job respond). Job is, apparently, sufficiently humbled after the Almighty himself has confronted him in Chaps. 38–41.

An Evaluation of Elihu

Many people consider the Elihu speeches to be decidedly inferior to the rest of the book. They think the book of Job would be better off without them. Many others think that Elihu is rather harmless, no better or worse than the other three counselors. His intrusion at the end really does not add very much, but it doesn't really hurt either. It is as if we added a fourth cycle to what we already had. Sooner or later the counselors will have to shut up and we can get on to the conclusion of the book when God speaks. Elihu delays that a bit but doesn't really change anything. Still others appreciate Elihu, to a greater or lesser degree, even to the point of arguing for his existence in the mind of the original author. Some appreciate Elihu because of the intellectual content of his message. They think that he really does add something to the debate about why humans, even ones like Job, sometimes suffer, and how God relates to such unpleasant human experiences. Others speak well of Elihu because they think he plays an important role in preparing Job for God, addressing Job in a way that helps him out of his rut of pitiful self-preoc-cupation, so that he can hear what God had probably been trying to say to him all along.

Let us look a little more carefully at an evaluation of Elihu from both these perspectives—the theological content and the psychological (or spiritual) process.

1. Is there anything new on the level of content?

The writer of the Elihu speeches probably thought that he was providing something new. The prose introduction and opening speech by Elihu, in which he is critical of what has been said so far and waxes (not so eloquently) about his need to proclaim his own words, implies that there is more to say, that the argument has not been settled, that further theological discussion of this matter will clarify the issues. This sounds like someone who thinks he has a new word which will be of benefit to all of us impoverished (up till now) readers.

But is there anything new? The heart of Elihu's message is probably in 33:13-30 and 36:8-15. His theological understanding of suffering emphasizes divine justice (the doctrine of retribution), the fact that all human beings are sinners, and the belief that God can use our suffering for our own benefit if we will but heed the message which God intends for us. On a theological level, those are not bad explanations of the "Why?" of suffering. Many people have been helped by thoughts such as these, singly or in combination. If Elihu were speaking to a seminar on the interpretation of suffering rather than to a suffering human being like Job, he might have been fairly effective.

Even if we grant some value, in certain situations, to his message, does Elihu really say anything that has not been said already by one or more of the previous counselors? I think not. In fact, most of Elihu's basic message had already been said by Eliphaz before we got to Chap. 6. Perhaps Elihu carries further the suggestion that God's chastening is a benefit to us, but Eliphaz had at least opened that possibility already in 5:17ff. Those who like this explanation of suffering tend to like Elihu. In commenting on Elihu's words we were reminded many times that he is very similar to Eliphaz; one would almost conclude that the Elihu writer was a rather strong admirer of Eliphaz (in spite of his negative comments about him and the others). Perhaps he did not think Eliphaz went far enough. But Elihu's extension of the argument does not really deepen it or bring something new. It only prolongs the discussion of what was already there.

2. Does Elihu help Job move through his process of suffering?

There were some positive factors in Elihu's approach to Job. He had paid close attention to what Job said and then presented Job's words back to him so that they could be looked at carefully. He did promise that he would be impartial (32:21) and he would not talk down to Job (33:5-7). Unfortunately, as it turned out, Elihu used Job's own words as weapons against him rather than as thoughts and feelings to be aired and discussed. We have already noted Elihu's failure to live up to his ideal of impartiality (at least in any dispute between God and humans), and his efforts at humility were quickly shoved aside by his pompous and pontifical fascination with his own importance and exalted wisdom. It seems that those who regard Elihu in a favorable light with respect to his relational skills look only at Elihu's statement of his intention and neglect to examine the way he actually dealt with Job.

For Elihu, as for the other counselors, Job's suffering is an intellectual problem to be solved, not a tragedy in which one ministers. Elihu is very heavy-handed (some call him confrontational) in calling Job to account for things which he might have said out of great duress. There is no room for human lament, no willingness to understand why the sufferer is saying such things, but rather a compulsion to correct and criticize what sounds like impiety or bad theology. Protection of God's attributes, particularly omnipotence and justice, takes top priority.

One might argue that this objection to Elihu might be true if we were talking about the early stages of Job's suffering. By the time Elihu comes along, some would argue that this has been going on long enough and what Job really needs is a good, hard-nosed dose of reality in which he is made responsible and is not allowed to retreat into hostility toward others and wallow in self-pity. *If* that is what he needed, then that is certainly what he received from Elihu.

I am still not convinced. I think that Elihu was not able to help Job in the process of moving beyond blaming to a more positive acceptance of his suffering and willingness to live with unanswered questions. Though the text does not report Job's response to Elihu, it seems to me that Elihu only rigidified Job's situation by antagonizing him, forcing him into a corner, zealously condemning him in order to protect God. So both Elihu and Job are still playing the game, "Whose fault is it?" They are both caught in the trap of insisting that there must be an intellectual answer. And so Elihu's use of a hymn which extols God's wisdom in nature and points to human inability to comprehend all the mysteries of the creation can be seen as a device to quiet Job, to stifle his honest questions. If Elihu had been able to accept such words of caution about the limitation of human wisdom for himself, then he would have much more credibility when he asks Job to relinquish his quest for answers and submit humbly to the power and mystery of God. Maybe, after God speaks, this will be possible.

7

God's Speeches and the Epilog (Job 38-42)

The time has finally arrived. Job has long been hoping for a direct word from God. Very early in the book (perhaps even before Eliphaz finished his first presentation in Chaps. 4–5), Job had come to the conclusion that his friends would be no help in making sense out of his suffering. His only chance lay with God. If only God would make clear to him why all this was happening to him. If only God would explain it. In some ways, Job was terrified by the thought of trying to argue his case before Almighty God (e.g., 9:2; 13:13-15), but he saw no other alternative. Job thought his situation before God was similar to a defendant before a judge. If Job could make a strong enough case for his innocence, he could be acquitted (e.g., 23:3-7). If God reveals some secret indictment previously unknown to Job, it would be better to get it out into the light (e.g., 31:35-37). Job cannot stand not knowing. The unanswered "Why?" questions burn deep within him and he cannot rest until he has some answers.

God does appear to Job. His hope is fulfilled. God does talk to him. The silence is broken. But the conversation will be on God's terms, not Job's. It is God who sets the agenda for this meeting. God does not answer Job's questions. When this magnificent experience of encounter with God is over, Job still does not know why he suffered; he still does not know about the part Satan had played in this drama; he remains in the dark with regard to most of his questions. In common with most people who suffer, Job does not receive any adequate explanation of the disaster that entered his life. He is, however, now aware of God's presence in a new and profound way. His remaining unanswered questions become tolerable in the context of a restored relationship of trust in God.

God's First Speech (Chapters 38–39)

Many scholars have remarked about the beauty of God's first speech. It is a wonderfully descriptive account of God's creative activity. In the first part of this speech, God asks Job if he could do the mighty acts that God has done in making the earth and sea and sky and ensuring that everything operates in good order. In the second part of the first speech, God speaks about his concern for his animals, the delight which he takes in them, and the sustaining care with which he attends to every creature that he has made. Throughout this speech, the reader detects a note of sarcasm as God directs pointed questions at Job—questions that are meant to make obvious the inability of humans to know and do what is possible only for God. Some students of Job have not liked the way God speaks to Job. God seems harsh, even cruel, as he ridicules Job's pretensions in desiring to know the unknowable. Some have remarked that God should be a bit more gentle with Job after all that Job has been through, especially in light of God's own complicity in the onset of Job's troubles.

"Job, do you know how to create a world?" (38:1-38)

The first three verses are a direct challenge to Job to prepare himself for what God will say. God is called "the LORD" (i.e., the Hebrew letters *yhwh)* in 38:1. For whatever reason, God's name, *yhwh,* is used in the prolog and epilog and God speeches, but nowhere else in the book of Job—not in the dialog between Job and his three friends and not in the monolog of Elihu.

God speaks from the whirlwind. It is rather common to describe appearances of God (theophanies) in mighty storms, often accompanied by thunder, lightning, clouds, and wind (see, for example, Pss. 18:7-15; 50:3; Ezek. 1:4; Nah. 1:3; and Zech. 9:14). A whirlwind is a good image for God's presence. The wind, like God, is a powerful force which we can feel and the effects of which we can see, but we cannot see the wind itself. The clouds which often accompany the wind both reveal and obscure. We can see the cloud (and know God is there—as in the pillar of cloud that led Israel in the wilderness) but we cannot see into the cloud (and, therefore cannot penetrate God's mystery).

Verses 2 and 3 are addressed to Job, not Elihu, even though in the present form of the book, Elihu has been the last to speak. God's very first words are confrontational. Who is this Job who questions God's plans for the world with ignorant words? Job should prepare himself for an onslaught of questions. Way back in 9:3-12, Job had a premonition that it would be like this. But it is too late to turn back. Job wanted to hear from God and now he has no choice but to listen.

God proceeds to describe the task of creating the world. Where was Job when all this was done? What does he know about the details of measuring the earth's foundations, shutting up the unruly sea, exploring the waters under the sea, sending the snow and rain, or ordering the movement of the stars? All these questions are meant to arouse in Job a feeling of humility, incapability: "Of course, I can't do that." Along with these questions which point to Job's inadequacy are other questions which ask, "Who is actually taking care of all these details?" The answer, of course, is God. Humans can't do it—but God can. Humans can't understand it—but God can. There is a gap between human and divine. That is the way it is. Humans were not created to be God. Only God can be God, and if Job will accept that, his life will be a whole lot easier.

As we read through this section, we are struck by the sense of order in creation. God knew exactly what he was doing when he made the world. The foundation was carefully measured (v. 5). Sea is contained, limited to certain areas, not allowed beyond God's boundaries so that we humans can be safe from sea's fury (vv. 8-11). The light of dawn exposes the wicked so they cannot carry out their evil deeds (vv. 12-15). God is the only one capable of comprehending the expanse of the earth, observing all that happens (v. 18). Rain and snow and hail are all stored until needed and then are dispensed by God (vv. 22-23, 25-28). The stars of the heavens move according to set times and seasons (vv. 31-33). In short, God tells Job that "all is in good order, I am running things just fine, and, even though you don't understand all the details, you can rest comfortably in the assurance that I will take care of what is beyond your capacity to understand or control."

"Job, can you rule the animal kingdom?" (38:39—39:30)

Now the subject changes from geology, astronomy, and meteorology to biology. God has spoken of earth and sea and sky but now God speaks with pride of his animals. Several different species are singled out for special attention. In the background is the ongoing question to Job about his inability to create, control, or provide for these magnificent representatives of God's creatures. It is clear that God has made them, God takes great pleasure in them, and God accounts for each and every one of them—even the baby mountain goats on faraway mountain peaks where mere mortals cannot even see them (39:1-3).

This section can be further divided into smaller parts which describe the following animals and birds: lions (38:39-40) and ravens (38:41); the mountain goats (39:1-4); the wild ass (39:5-8); the wild ox (39:9-12); the ostrich (39:13-18); the horse (39:19-25); and the hawk or eagle (39:26-30). God provides food for the lions and ravens. God even knows the gestation period of each mountain goat and observes its birth. God has given the wild ass freedom and a place to roam. Humans cannot tame the wild ox (though it is implied that God can).

The passage on the ostrich is peculiar for several reasons. There are no questions directed at Job as in the discourses on all the other animals. God is mentioned in the third person (v. 17) rather than the first person. Also, the Septuagint (the ancient Greek translation of the Old Testament) omits the whole section on the ostrich. For these reasons, some scholars have thought that this section is a later addition, or is at least out of place. On the other hand, it is a delightful passage and certainly adds to the image of a God who loves and cares for his animals. The Hebrew at the beginning (v. 13) and end (v. 18) is very difficult. Probably, v. 13 is a comment on the uselessness of the ostrich's wings for flight. Another problem with the ostrich is its stupidity as a mother, leaving eggs on the ground to be trampled. Interestingly, God takes responsibility for making the ostrich stupid (v. 17). But, whatever disparaging remarks we may make about the ostrich, when she decides to run, she can laugh even at a horse and its rider (v. 18). One can almost detect a sense of humor in this picture of the ostrich, as if created by God for comic relief.

As our text returns to the kind of questions that were missing in the ostrich passage, God asks Job whether he gives the horse its strength or makes it leap like a locust (vv. 19-20). As before, the obvious answer is no for Job and yes for God. The section on the horse (vv. 19-25) is much praised and thought by many to be the best of these subsections on the animals.

The final example of animal life which God holds up before Job is the bird of prey—the hawk in v. 26 and the eagle in vv. 27-30. Of course it is not by Job's wisdom that the hawk soars (v. 26) or at Job's command that the eagle makes its nest high in the mountains (v. 27). (Contrast the location of the eagle's nest with that of the ostrich.) As with the other examples, God has made his creatures with beauty, strength, courage, and instincts for survival. God has given them places to live and run or fly according to God's will for them.

Job's First Response:
"OK, I'll Be Quiet" (40:1-5)

There is a pause. God asks Job if he wants to continue the argument. Job has been so eager to find fault with the way God is running the world. If he has any answer to what God has been saying, let him speak up now (40:2).

Job is overwhelmed. Certainly, he is aware that God has not answered his questions, that he does not know why he is suffering, that there has been no public accounting of his guilt or innocence. God has side-stepped his questions, pointing to the wonders of nature and avoiding issues of God's justice (though we should note God's concern in 38:13, 15 to curb the wicked) and Job's suffering. Yet Job decides that he had better be quiet. There is nothing he can say. It would be foolish to try to push his case. He has said a lot already, but now he will quit talking (vv. 4-5).

Is Job yet satisfied? Has the encounter with God somehow moved him from his fault-finding position to one of acceptance and trust even in the face of unexplained suffering? When he says he will speak no more, is he merely bowing to pressure, feeling bullied and intimidated by God's display of power? If Job has now gained some serenity in his suffering, then why does God need to speak again? Is this overkill on God's part or does Job still need more convincing? These are difficult questions to answer. Some scholars think that the first speech of God accomplished what was necessary. Job yielded, and the second speech of God is superfluous at best, and, at worst, just plain cruel. Therefore, they conclude that for this and other reasons (it seems of inferior literary quality), the second speech of God is not part of the original book of Job.[30]

Though one cannot be certain about such things, in this case it seems best to take the God speeches as they are. As Job's calamities came on him in two stages, so perhaps there is an intended symmetry in the way that God's speaking to Job, and Job's acceptance of what God says, also comes in two stages. After the first speech, Job is cowed into submission, but it is not yet fully his own position. Rather, he feels pressured from the outside. The insight of his own human limitations has not quite penetrated to his being. It is not yet completely congenial to him. He is still fighting it and holding out for something else. So he can use another dose of God's medicine.

God's Second Speech (40:6—41:34)

"All right, Job. You run the show" (40:6-14)

God again speaks from the whirlwind (v. 6) and tells Job to brace himself for another round of questions (v. 7). God accuses Job of condemning God in order to put himself in the right (v. 8). As long as one is locked into a courtroom mentality where someone must be guilty, as long as the question of blame is foremost, then Job is caught in the dilemma of blaming either himself or God. The traditional religious view of his day, so faithfully represented by his four counselors, is that humans are to blame for the suffering of the world. God is good and just, so it could not be he. People are the source of suffering. Job had resisted that conclusion because of his own integrity, which did not allow himself to wallow in guilt and confess to sins which he did not think he had committed. God recognizes that Job, in order to protect himself, had blamed God. That is not a good alternative to self-blame because it makes God look unjust and cruel. Though he maintained his own integrity, Job lost his confidence in a good God. What Job needs is not to go back to blaming himself but rather to move beyond his fixation with finding fault toward a willingness to leave such questions unanswered. He needs to let the questions drop so that he can again begin to trust God without having to choose the alternative of heaping guilt on himself.

Since Job has complained about God's execution of justice, God invites Job to try it himself. If he doesn't like the way God rules, let him do it himself. Let him see if he can achieve perfect justice in the world, bringing low the proud and destroying the wicked (vv. 11-13). If Job can pull that off, God will be the first to acknowledge that Job has the power to gain victory over evil.

These are fascinating words from God. We wish that we could hear the tone of voice as God invites Job to maintain justice in the world. Is there sarcasm here? "OK, wise guy, if you think you're so smart, you try it." God has earlier spoken of building the world and setting times and maneuvering the stars and sending the rain—all tasks impossible for humans—but maybe the execution of justice is the most difficult work of all. Humbling the proud and bringing recompense to the wicked are tasks so difficult that even God must work hard at them and is not always apparently successful (at least not from our human perspective). It may be that God, in this passage, is not only pointing out human limitations (as God has been doing already in these speeches) but is also admitting that it is hard to be God. Some have seen in this response to Job a painful acknowledgment from God that sometimes justice is hard to achieve, especially in a world filled with proud and wicked human beings who continually rebel against God's will. Nevertheless, it is clear that humans cannot achieve justice by themselves. Our only hope for justice is to look to God.[31]

The rest of God's second speech is composed of two sections, each a detailed discussion of a huge beast (either real or mythological), whose ferocity and power cannot be contained by human effort. The first is Behemoth (40:15-24) and the second is Leviathan (Chap. 41). Though somewhat similar to the descriptions of animals in the first speech, these sections are considerably different. They are longer, especially regarding Leviathan. They are generally considered to be of lower quality than the poetry of Chap. 39. And, if Behemoth and Leviathan are real animals (or modeled after actual beasts), they probably are the hippopotamus and crocodile, animals found in Egypt, not Palestine. But all the animals mentioned in God's first speech are found in Palestine. These differences have reinforced the hypothesis of some scholars that the second speech of God is inferior and unnecessary and should not be considered part of the original book of Job.

"Behold the mighty Behemoth" (40:15-24)

Though Behemoth eats grass like an ox, he is much more powerful than any domesticated animal (v. 15). The strength of his body is obvious to anyone who looks, comparable to cedar or bronze or iron (vv. 16-18). The meaning of v. 19 is uncertain, but may refer to Behemoth as *first* with regard to awesomeness and admirability or *first* in the sense of being created first. (Genesis 1:24 mentions "cattle" as the first animals created. The Hebrew word for "cattle" is *b^e hēmāh,* which is the singular form of the word *b^e hē- môth.*) The *sword* may refer to teeth or tusks which Behemoth uses as weapons and which contribute to the creature's ferocity. Verses 21-23 sound like the habitat and activity of a hippopotamus. Behemoth is not frightened even in turbulent waters. The mention of Jordan (in v. 23) may be symbolic for a rapidly descending stream since, as stated, there are no creatures like this in Palestine.

The main point for Job comes in v. 24. Can a human being go hunting with hooks or snare for the likes of Behemoth? It is another rhetorical question. The answer is expected to be no. Human beings have no chance against a monstrous beast like this. While looking at the Leviathan passage, we shall return to the question whether these are real, though terrifying, animals or imaginative descriptions (though based on perceptions of real animals) of supernatural (mythological) monsters who represent the power of evil in the world.

"Can you handle Leviathan?" (41:1-34)

The word *Leviathan* is used several times in the Bible to designate a sea monster, a serpent that personifies the power of evil. In Job 3:8, Job speaks of magicians who have the power to raise up Leviathan. Psalm 74:14 tells us that God has crushed Leviathan, and Isa. 27:1 promises that God will come one day to slay Leviathan (i.e., to destroy evil). Psalm 104:26 reminds us that even Leviathan is God's creation, put in the sea to frolic there. Other biblical passages talk about a serpent (e.g., Job 26:13) or Rahab (Isa. 51:9) or the Sea (as Job 7:12) in ways similar to these references to Leviathan. With this biblical tradition in mind, it is possible that the author intended to speak of a supernatural, cosmic evil power and not merely a crocodile, though the description of the creature sounds much like a crocodile. It is as if the poet begins with the most fearsome creatures known on the earth and then projects to imagine such dangerous, ugly, horrifying beasts on a supernatural level. We humans are helpless even against the earthly forms of these monsters. How much more so against their mythological counterparts?

God asks Job if he can catch Leviathan (v. 1), tame him, and teach him to do tricks like a pet (vv. 2-5), or take him to market to sell him there a piece at a time (v. 6). Don't believe it, says God. If you lay hands on him, that will be a battle you will not wage a second time (v. 8). No human is able to stand before Leviathan (v. 10). The mere sight of him drains one of courage (v. 9).

The main point has already been made by vv. 9-10. No human can survive in a battle with Leviathan. But the passage goes on to describe in greater detail the appearance of Leviathan (vv. 12-24). In vv. 18-21, we are told that he breathes smoke and fire. Leviathan is more like the dragons from our fairy tales than a mere crocodile. That is, this beast represents more than an animal, no matter how big and mean that beast is. There are no weapons that can subdue him (vv. 26-28). There is no other creature like him on earth. He is kingly and without fear (vv. 33-34). Nothing that is created—human or beast—can rival him for supremacy. Only God can do that.

Both these figures, Behemoth and Leviathan, represent the enormity of evil that is loose in the world. If we had to face such enemies on our own, we would have no chance whatsoever. But we can have hope, because even these fearsome beings are under God's control. They are God's creatures and cannot overstep the limits which God has placed on them. There is still an ambiguity here, a puzzlement why God allows these creatures to exist and have the freedom to bring us harm. It is the same problem we had in Chaps. 1–2 when we wondered why God let Satan hurt Job. It is the same question we ask from a Christian perspective when we try to understand why the devil is still alive if he has been slain by Jesus Christ. The imagery of these creatures, probably meant to be supernatural, though their description is based on real animals, reminds us that there is evil out there, and that without God's help we are totally vulnerable, but with God's help the ultimate victory is ours.

Job's Second Response:
"Now My Eye Sees Thee" (42:1-6)

We return to a passage which we examined as a way of dealing with some introductory matters in Chap. 1. The inconsistency between a Job who is blameless and a Job who needs to repent has provided some of the argument for those who would separate the prose portions (prolog and epilog) from the rest of the book. Verse 6 has provided an interesting look at one of the innumerable textual problems in the book of Job. Perhaps Job does not "despise" (or "reject") *himself* at all, but rather the *words* he has been saying or the complaining and blaming *rut* in which he has been stuck. Though not suffering because of his sin, he has, nevertheless, reacted to his suffering in ways that are best left behind.

Some change has come to Job. He now "sees" (that is, *experiences*) God in a way that he had not done before. He knows he has uttered words that he did not understand (v. 3). Now, in contrast to his mood after God's first speech, he seems finally ready to let go of the questions and trust God (v. 2). A few have wondered whether Job is satisfied even now. He asked God for an explanation and received an overwhelming show of God's power and human weakness. Is that a help to Job? He already knew that God was powerful. His problem was that he did not know whether God could be trusted and whether God still cared about him. Most scholars agree that God's presence was what Job most needed, that he now knew that God was there even in his suffering, and that the miseries in his life were not evidence of God's abandonment. The message is that God is present in our suffering, not that God answers all of our questions. Job is like sufferers of all ages for whom explanations remain elusive. But if God's presence is known, the need for specific answers greatly diminishes and the suffering becomes tolerable.

When reading this passage, note that v. 3a and v. 4 are not the words of Job. Verse 3a is nearly the same as God's opening word to Job in 38:2. Verse 4 recalls the divine questioning in 38:3 and 40:7. For some reason, God's words of challenge are juxtaposed with Job's confession. Job is now fully responding to God (he had done so only partially in 40:3-5).

The Epilog (42:7-17)

We now return to the ancient story of Job, written in prose, for a final resolution of Job's situation.

"God's judgment on Eliphaz, Bildad, and Zophar" (42:7-9)

After talking to Job, God turns to Eliphaz (we haven't heard from him for a long time) and gives him a message to pass on to the other two counselors

(v. 7). God is angry because Job's three friends did not speak the truth about God but Job did speak the truth (v. 7, 8b). This word from God has been rather confusing to students of Job in the light of what we have heard from God in the previous few chapters. God had seemed to scold Job for speaking words without knowledge (38:2), for being a faultfinder (40:1), and for condemning God in order to justify himself (40:8). What, then, does it mean that Job has spoken the truth in contrast to the three counselors? Part of the difficulty may be resolved if one accepts that the author of most of the book of Job used an old tale (the prolog and epilog) which was not changed sufficiently to harmonize with everything that the poet says in the rest of the book. Further, God's commendation of Job and anger with Eliphaz may be due primarily to their understanding of divine retribution. Eliphaz and the others had insisted that every example of suffering can be understood as punishment for sins committed by that individual sufferer. Job contended throughout the book that, even though we may wish the world worked in such an orderly way, it does not. Sometimes innocent people suffer, and Job presents himself as the best example of that reality. On this issue—the inadequacy of the doctrine of retribution to explain all suffering—Job is indeed right and his friends are wrong. Job may have been wrong in his accusations to God, but on this issue he was right.

God tells Eliphaz, Bildad, and Zophar to offer a sacrifice to atone for their incorrect theology and poor treatment of Job (v. 8). But the sacrifice, in itself, will not be sufficient unless Job, God's servant, prays for them. If Job prays on their behalf, God will listen. They do as they are told, and the Lord accepts Job's prayer (v. 9). There is a lovely irony here. The one whom the comforters had imagined to be a hopeless sinner worthy of his punishment becomes the righteous one who prays on their behalf. The one whom they came to comfort is now the one who is able to bring comfort to them. The one whom they urged to confess his sins before God in order to be relieved of his suffering now becomes the one who asks God to remove their sins. Many of the great Old Testament characters were noted for their intercession on behalf of others: Abraham (Gen. 18:23ff.; 20:7), Moses (32:11ff.; Num. 21:7; Deut. 9:20), Samuel (1 Sam. 12:19,23), Amos (Amos 7:2-6), and Jeremiah (Jer. 37:3) are some of the best examples. Job himself is remembered as a righteous intercessor, along with Noah and Daniel, in Ezek. 14:14,20.

It is interesting to note that Elihu is not mentioned here. Most would take that as further evidence that Elihu is a later addition to the book. Those who particularly like the message and style of Elihu could argue that he is not mentioned because he is not to be reprimanded like the others inasmuch as his word was true. He is, however, not commended either.

The Lord restores Job's fortunes (42:10-17)

The Lord restored Job's fortunes, but, it is interesting to note, this came after Job had prayed for his friends (v. 10). Perhaps we should not make too much of this but it may be very significant that Job begins to ascend out of the depths once he has looked away from his own despair and has interceded on behalf of others. There may well be something symbolic in Job's ability now to focus attention on the needs of others and not be preoccupied exclusively with his own pain.

The Lord gave Job twice what he had before (vv. 10b, 12). His latter days were even better than the beginning (v. 12a). Only in the number of children is there no doubling. The new family is exactly the size of the old—seven sons and three daughters (v. 13). Property and material possessions can be restored, even doubled. Dead children cannot be replaced. They are gone forever. Even in Job's newly restored state, one could guess that the pain of their loss would remain. It would be insensitive to double the size of his new family as if they, too, are a commodity that can be replaced or even increased. Job does receive a new family. God blesses him with posterity. But the memory of what was lost will remain.

All his kinfolk and former acquaintances now came to show sympathy for Job and to comfort him for the evil that the Lord had brought upon him (v. 11). They even brought him gifts of money and gold rings (v. 11b). Where were these people when Job really needed them? Now that his life has improved, everything is looking up, and his wealth has been restored, he is suddenly surrounded by empathetic well-wishers. Had these people been waiting for his recovery before they showed their faces? Why had they stayed away when Job felt so isolated and lonely in the midst of his torment? Whatever we may say about the ineptitude of Eliphaz, Bildad, and Zophar, at least they came to see Job in his time of need.

Verse 11 indicates that in the minds of Job's family and friends, as well as in Job's own understanding, God had brought the evil upon Job. Now they know that it was not because Job was a bad person who deserved it. But, from their theological perspective, nothing happens that is not God's doing. As Job said at the beginning, the Lord gives and the Lord takes away (1:21b).

The text never says that Job was healed of his physical illness. Perhaps it is assumed. Since everything else was restored to him, probably his health was also renewed. But it is interesting to think about what difference it would make if Job was still sick, a chronic sufferer, even though living to 140 years and again thriving financially. Not everyone has such a happy ending as Job. Would it have been enough for Job to be assured of God's presence and care for him (as at the end of God's speeches)? Would that have sustained him even if his life had remained a constant battle with suffering? It has been enough for many sufferers who have found that God was with them in the depths even though the suffering did not go away.

Job's daughters are singled out for special attention (vv. 14-15). They are known throughout the land for their beauty. Further, we are told that they, as well as the sons, had an inheritance from their father (v. 15b). It was unusual for a woman to inherit property in those times. According to Num. 27:1-11, daughters could inherit if there were no sons to receive their father's property. But in Job's case, there were seven sons. In our day, it is tempting to look at a passage like this and see it as an early glimmer of hope for equal rights for women—certainly not the common practice, but a reminder that sex roles are not as stereotyped in the Bible as we might think.

Job lived to a ripe old age and saw several generations of descendants (v. 16). He had a reprieve. The death which seemed imminent during his time of suffering was postponed for many, many years. But he did die. When death comes to one full of days, old and respected, surrounded by loving offspring who will carry on the family name and tradition, it is less tragic than in other circumstances. But it is death, nonetheless, the end of existence as we know it. Job, as we all, must die. But then what? Is there a resurrection? Does life continue beyond the grave? As we have seen the book of Job is, at best, ambiguous about this hope. And, in many passages, it seems to affirm that this life is the only life we have. We Christians add our own beliefs about this to the book of Job. In fact, the Septuagint (transmitted by Christians as their version of the Old Testament) adds a note at the end of the book indicating that Job will be among those whom the Lord will raise from the dead.

THEOLOGICAL AND PASTORAL CONCERNS

1. The message of the speeches of God

The speeches of God are the climax. Everything points toward them as the heart of the message of the whole book. If that is the case, as it seems to be, then what do we learn, finally, about suffering from the speeches of God? There is much difference of opinion here, though most will agree on the following two points:

(a) There is a gap between human and divine understanding which cannot be bridged. Human beings cannot know everything. That is simply the way things are, though human beings have a hard time living with the unknown, the mystery, the unanswered question. At some point, we humans need to stop banging our heads against the wall, expending great energy and experiencing enormous frustration, and accept the reality of human limitations.

But it is hard to do that if we have a glimmer of distrust in our hearts and minds about God and God's activity in the world. If we are not sure about God, then we are not so willing to leave the unknown in God's hands.

(b) The relationship with God is more important than answers to our "Why?" questions. When we know God is good and caring and involved in our life, we can accept the fact of our own vulnerability. If we do not trust God, we fight all the harder to defend ourselves and find our own answers.

Job's problem was not his lack of understanding why he was suffering, though he had thought that it was. Few humans are ever satisfied with answers to such questions. His deeper problem was that his relationship of intimacy and trust with God had been severely distorted. He needed to know that God still cared for him and had not abandoned him, as could have been evidenced by his terrible suffering. Somehow, God's speeches had the effect of reaching Job on the relational level, the spiritual level. Though questions remained, Job's trust in God had returned. Now the hard questions of cause and effect faded into the background. God loved him. That was the primary "answer." All other questions are now shifted to a secondary level.

So, for sufferers in our own day, the real need may be for a strengthening of faith to bear the suffering, though they will pose questions as if they are dealing with an intellectual problem for which a correct answer can be found. What most sufferers need is a visit from God, some words of confrontation and comfort, a feeling of God's presence, permission to "let go" of pretenses about wisdom and immortality and power, the willingness to let God do what we can't do. But how does a sufferer move to that point? Many are still stuck where Job was in Chap. 23, looking for God here and there but not finding God. Faith cannot be produced on the spot by an act of will. We humans cannot control the time or the place when God will meet us at a profound level and let us know that it is all right because God knows what we are enduring and God is in charge. Yet Job is an example to us, a model of one who sought God with integrity in his time of trouble, who did not give up in disgust or despair, and to whom God came with an assurance that only God can give. Though we cannot manipulate God, we have the promise that God will come to meet us in our own times of trouble.

2. The importance of creation imagery in God's speeches

The content of God's address to Job was heavily loaded with descriptions of God's creation—earth, sky, sea, and animals. This language was meant to have an effect on Job, to move him from his stubborn pursuit of "Why?" questions to a faith able to live with mystery. There are a number of reasons why creation imagery could be helpful to a sufferer like Job.

The Bible presents two main ways of knowing God. One is by looking at what God has done for us in history (the exodus, return from exile, recovery from an illness, return of prosperity, and so on). The event which indicates that God is at work in the world may be a momentous deed of salvation to which the whole society pays homage (e.g., the exodus) or it may be a personal story of deliverance from danger or illness or poverty. The other way of knowing God's presence in the world is to look at the creation. The sun, the moon, the stars, the beauty of cloud and flower all attest to a power which was able to make such things and synchronize them so that they all work together. Hymns in the book of Psalms praise God for deeds done on our behalf in history *and* for the wonders of the created order.

At some times, God is seen clearly in the recitation of history, in the telling of our story of God's involvement in our lives. At other times, when things are not going so well—when the enemy has just taken over the city, when the temple has been demolished, when the son for whom prayers were offered died anyway, when a good man like Job suffers—then one wonders whether God is at work in our lives. "Sure, God, you saved the ancient Israelites at the Sea of Reeds, but what have you done for me lately?" At such times, creation imagery can be helpful, turning our attention away from an area where it is momentarily difficult to praise God, and toward an area where we may still see evidence of God's work. Such an approach would seem to be fitting for a person like Job.

Pondering the creation in its immensity and order and mystery can have reassuring, yet humbling, effects on us. Its order can be a comfort to us. Even though our personal world is "going to hell in a basket," the order of creation continues. The sun rises and sets, seasons come and go, the clouds race across the sky, the bird sings its song. The regularity and continuity of nature can be comforting. The God who watches even for the individual sparrow or knows when the mountain goat will deliver its young must be a God who will also take care of us. Many sufferers have been profoundly helped by being in touch with nature, often in a favorite spot by the lake or in the garden or viewing the mountains. Even the existence of God's wonderful animals is a positive influence for many, whether they are observed in a picture book, or in the national park, or at the zoo, or as pets within our own home.

Viewing the creation can also have the effect of humbling us, letting us know we are not the center of the universe and our personal suffering is not like the end of God's world. The old cliché is still true. When we look at the stars on a clear summer night, we do feel small and insignificant. We cannot run the universe. We are dependent on a higher being who is able to understand the mysteries which, in some ways, seem only to be multiplied by the complexity of modern science.

3. God finally breaks the silence

Why did God wait so long to speak? As early as the first cycle (e.g., 13:3), Job expressed his need for an audience with God. Like so many sufferers (as attested in many lament psalms, for example), Job's suffering was compounded by God's silence and, with the silence, a sense of God's absence. If Job could have been helped by a word from God, a personal audience with God, why did God hold back, prolonging the time of Job's suffering?

Perhaps it is not God's hesitation but Job's inability to hear. Perhaps God has been there all the time, trying to speak, patiently waiting until Job has had his time to complete his case and fully express his complaint. Elihu had reminded Job that God does indeed answer our prayers (33:13ff.), though we are often unable to perceive it. Later, Elihu had more to say in defense of God's apparent silence in the face of sufferers' cries for help (35:9-16). Certainly, there is some truth to what Elihu says, but he seems too eager to exonerate God as he puts the entire responsibility for God's silence on the lack of sincerity of the cry for help ("Surely God does not hear an empty cry," 35:13a).

There is no point in blaming the sufferer for his or her inability to hear God's reply and feel God's presence. Certainly it is not lack of sincerity on the part of the one asking for a word from God. There is mystery here. One cannot control the moment when God speaks, the feeling of "blessed assurance," the clarity and insight that had been absent, the certainty that God is present no matter how difficult and precarious the journey through the dark valley. One can only thank God when that moment comes, as it did with Job. Rather than wonder why it didn't come sooner, we should think of this section of Job as a promise: "No matter how hopeless it may seem to you today, take heart. God indeed will come to meet you in your suffering."

4. God's treatment of Job

There are several ways to understand the intention of God in the speeches of God. We have chosen the approach, followed in one way or another by most Job scholars, that God's approach to Job was positive, that Job needed this kind of confrontation with God to snap him out of his rut, that God was first of all concerned for Job and was not pulling a power play in order to get Job to shut up. The positive effect on Job (e.g., 42:5) and the way the church and the Jewish community have understood these passages lend support to that point of view.

Still, there are those who do not like the image of God as presented in Chaps. 38–41. They see God as a bully, intimidating Job into submission, talking to Job in a sarcastic, humiliating manner. They think this is the behavior of a God who is more concerned to protect himself from human questioning than to help the one who suffers.

There is some uncertainty here, but the evidence seems greater on the side of those who see God's treatment of Job as a positive, necessarily confrontational approach, for Job's own good. As in our picture of God in Chaps. 1–2, not all difficulties can be swept away. But we should leave the book of Job knowing that God is on our side and not against us.

5. Realistic and unrealistic hopes in Job

Job has a happy ending. God vindicates him, makes his three counselors grovel a little, and restores his wealth and reputation. But does life always work that way? To say that it does is to say that the doctrine of retribution is right, after all. Job is finally rewarded for hanging in there when the going was rough, and now, since he is a good and contrite person (42:1-6), he receives his reward. It almost looks as if Job won the battle but lost the war. If the book is meant to show that simple-minded doctrines connecting our behavior with rewards or punishments are wrong, then the last chapter seems to let the doctrine of retribution sneak in the back door again. Many people who have agonized with Job throughout the book have felt betrayed by the way the book ends. The good are rewarded and the evil punished—just as in a grade B western movie.

Many who read the book of Job are lured into the idea that they too should have their losses restored, their illnesses cured, their broken relationships healed—especially if they have been good religious people. They set the epilog in Job alongside stories of Jesus healing those who have sufficient faith (e.g., Matt. 9:22, with parallels in Mark 5 and Luke 8), and they build up an expectation that that is the way it should work out in their lives. If God can heal the woman with a hemorrhage and Job, then why not them?

But the rest of the book of Job centers on the struggle with suffering of a good person who sees no reason for it and no end to it. Job has an important word for those whose suffering continues, whose lament is not over, who are not participants in a happy ending. The most important event for Job was God's coming to him—even more so than the story of his restoration. The latter is frosting on the cake, but Job, I think, would have been able to continue even if the events of 42:7-17 had never occurred.

Yet the story of the restoration is important. Suffering is never the final word. God will one day move to defeat suffering once and for all. The book of Job needs to include an account of God's action to heal and make right, especially because of God's involvement in the beginning of Job's suffering. From our Christian perspective, we could tell a story about God's vindication in the next life. But for the author of Job it must take place here and now or not at all. So it sounds a little simplistic, a little too pat, after the agonizing struggles of the rest of the book. But someone saw a need for a concluding story of God's victory over suffering in order to make the book complete.

We, too, hope for restoration in this life. But we must not be misled into thinking that whether or not it comes has something to do with our goodness or our faith. As with Job, good people do suffer, and some do not have a happy ending—not in this life anyway.

If our suffering remains, we still have hope. We hope that we, unlike Job, will be blessed with understanding and loving comforters who will listen to our pain without condemning us. We hope that God will let us know of God's existence, presence, and care. We hope that God will gain the ultimate victory over all that can harm us—if not in this world, then in the next. These hopes can sustain us as we continue our journey through this life toward an even brighter future with God.

Notes

1. See the discussion of textual and linguistic problems in Marvin Pope, *Job*, Anchor Bible (Garden City, N.Y.: Doubleday, 1965), pp. xxxix to xlv. A good presentation of the problems with the Septuagint of Job can be found in Marvin Pope's article, "Job, Book of," *IDB* 2:911-912, and in Robert Gordis, *The Book of God and Man: A Study of Job* (Chicago: University of Chicago Press, 1965), pp. 222-223. Most commentaries on Job will make some observations about the difficulty of the text.
2. Job 14:14 provides an interesting example of how the Septuagint (the ancient Greek translation) has modified the Hebrew text. Job asks, "If a man die, will he live again?" The Septuagint removes the question and has Job assert that man, in fact, will live again. Almost every modern English translation follows the Hebrew here rather than the Greek.
3. Dale Patrick makes a good case for this interpretation in his article, "The Translation of Job 42:6," *VT* 26 (1976): 369-371.
4. See John Briggs Curtis, "On Job's Response to Yahweh," *JBL* 98 (1979): 497-511.
5. It seems unlikely that, as Curtis suggests, Job is still dripping with hostility toward God at this stage of his story. Such an interpretation flies in the face of centuries of understanding about Job as taught by the Jewish and Christian communities. Neither is it necessary to think of Job as loathing himself, as if the only way to get right with God is to adopt an attitude of self-hatred. But Job does not like something about what he has been saying and doing. He wants to leave behind his negative attitudes, accusations toward God, preoccupation with self, and move on to a new level of trust in God. In interpreting a passage like this, surely our own piety has a great influence on our choice of the best way to understand it.
6. One can read discussions of the relationship between the prose and poetic sections in almost any commentary on Job. See, for example, Pope's article in *IDB*, p. 920; Samuel Terrien, *Job: Poet of Existence* (New York: Bobbs-Merrill, 1957), pp. 23-33; H. H. Rowley, *The Book of Job* (Grand Rapids; Eerdmans, 1980), pp.

8-12; and Samuel Terrien, "Introduction and Exegesis of Job," *IB* 3:884-888. An example of a more conservative approach which seeks to maintain as much unity as possible between the prose and poetry sections is Francis I. Anderson, *Job: An Introduction and Commentary* (Leicester: InterVarsity, 1976), pp. 20-21.

7. For further discussion of the Elihu question, see the commentaries by Pope, Rowley, Terrien, and Anderson. Gordis, in *The Book of God and Man,* presents the interesting, though not very convincing, theory that the Elihu speeches were added to the finished book of Job by the author himself—his own updating of his work from a later point in his life (pp. 110-114).

8. Questions of dating can be pursued in most commentaries on Job. See, for example, Pope, *IDB*, p. 914; Terrien, *IB* 3:888; Anderson, pp. 62-63; Rowley, p. 21; and Gordis, pp. 216-218.

9. The location of Uz is not known. There are a few biblical references to the name, but they are not consistent. See Rowley, p. 28.

10. There are good summaries of these ancient stories in Terrien, *IB* 3:879-884, and Pope, *Job,* pp. 1 to lxvi.

11. See the discussion of this in S. R. Driver and G. B. Gray, *A Critical and Exegetical Commentary on the Book of Job* (New York: Scribner's, 1921), 2:4-6. Note also the explanation given in Brown, Driver, Briggs, *A Hebrew and English Lexicon of the Old Testament* (Oxford: Clarendon, 1968), p. 139.

12. This is Rowley's position (p. 32).

13. Archibald MacLeish develops this theme in "God Has Need of Man," an essay in Nahum N. Glatzer, *The Dimensions of Job: A Study and Selected Readings* (New York: Schocken, 1969), pp. 278-286.

14. This factor is often included in arguments about dating.

15. On pp. 51-53 Rowley gives a good summary of the possibilities.

16. Again, note the discussion of this in Rowley, pp. 53-54.

17. Verse 14 is difficult to translate, but it is probably an accusation against Eliphaz for not showing kindness. See discussion of this verse by Rowley, pp. 61-62, and Terrien, *Job: Poet of Existence,* pp. 56-57.

18. The RSV translates "accuser," though the KJV and NIV have "Judge." The former seems preferable.

19. The RSV in v. 15a reads, "Behold he will slay me; I have no hope." The KJV had a much more pious translation, "Though he slay me, yet will I trust in him." In this context, the former seems more likely, since the mood is not one of acquiescence on Job's part. These differences reflect the two possibilities of reading either what was *written* in the Hebrew text (*lō'*—the negative) or what was suggested as the proper *reading* in the margin *lô*—"to him").

20. The JB translates it this way.

21. For a good discussion of a God who has passion and feelings about human beings, see Abraham Heschel, *The Prophets* (New York: Harper and Row, 1962). See also Terence Fretheim, *The Suffering of God* (Philadelphia: Fortress, 1984).

22. See Rowley, p. 157.

23. The JB rearranges the speeches at the end of the third cycle according to the principle that Job is the one who could be speaking in criticism of God's justice toward the wicked and the counselors are the ones who would be upholding the eventuality of retribution for the wicked.

24. For further discussion of this problem and a look at several theories of how to reorder Chaps. 24 through 27, see Rowley, pp. 167-178; Terrien, *IB*, p. 888; Pope, *IDB*, p. 919.

25. As Rowley, p. 172, and others.

26. As, for example, Pope in *IDB*, p. 921, and Rowley, p. 14.

27. Andersen argues consistently for the unity of authorship for the book of Job, and so is predisposed to see the value of Elihu's speeches as an integral part of the whole, creating "an interval of suspense against which the words of the Lord become all the more majestic" (p. 19). William Hulme, in *Dialogue in Despair* (Nashville: Abingdon, 1968), writing from the perspective of pastoral counseling, values the Elihu discourses as necessary for the transition from a defiant Job to a Job who is receptive to the divine revelation (p. 110).

28. See the translations in JB and TEV, which follow this line of thought.

29. See the discussion of this verse in Rowley, p. 208, and Pope, *Job,* p. 212.

30. As Rowley on p. 15 and p. 254.

31. Harold Kushner, in his popular book, *When Bad Things Happen to Good People* (New York: Schocken, 1981), makes much of Job 40:9-14, seeing this passage as perhaps the most important in the book (p. 43). He uses these verses to support his view that God does not control everything that happens in this world and should not, therefore, be blamed for all of our suffering.

Selected Bibliography

Andersen, Francis I. *Job: An Introduction and Commentary.* Leicester: InterVarsity, 1976.

Curtis, John Briggs. "On Job's Response to Yahweh." *JBL* 98 (1979): 497-511.

Driver, S. R. and Gray, G. B. *A Critical and Exegetical Commentary on the Book of Job.* International Critical Commentary. New York: Scribner's, 1921.

Fretheim, Terence. *The Suffering of God.* Philadelphia: Fortress, 1984.

Gordis, Robert. *The Book of God and Man: A Study of Job.* Chicago: University of Chicago Press, 1965.

Habel, Norman. *The Book of Job: A Commentary.* Philadelphia: Westminster, 1985.

Heschel, Abraham. *The Prophets.* New York: Harper & Row, 1962.

Hulme, William. *Dialogue in Despair.* Nashville: Abingdon, 1968.

Kushner, Harold. *When Bad Things Happen to Good People.* New York: Schocken, 1981.

MacLeish, Archibald. "God Has Need of Man." In *The Dimensions of Job: A Study and Selected Readings.* Edited by N. Glatzer. New York: Schocken, 1969.

Patrick, Dale. "The Translation of Job 42:6." *VT* 26 (1976): 369-371.

Pope, Marvin. *Job.* Anchor Bible. Garden City, N.Y.: Doubleday, 1965.

_____ . "Job, Book of." In *IDB*, 2:911-925. Nashville: Abingdon, 1962.

Rowley, H. H. *The Book of Job.* The New Century Bible Commentary. Grand Rapids: Eerdmans, 1980.

Simundson, Daniel J. *Faith under Fire: Biblical Interpretations of Suffering.* Minneapolis: Augsburg, 1980.

Terrien, Samuel. "Introduction and Exegesis of Job." In *IB*, vol. 3. Nashville: Abingdon, 1954.

_____ . *Job: Poet of Existence.* New York: Bobbs-Merrill, 1957.

Westermann, Claus. *The Structure of the Book of Job: A Form-Critical Analysis.* Philadelphia: Fortress, 1981.

Zucherman, B. "Job, Book of." In *IDBSup*, pp. 479-481. Nashville: Abingdon, 1976.